the Steps of our SAVIOUR

First published in 2011 by Striving Together Publications, a ministry of Lancaster Baptist Church, Lancaster, CA 93535. Striving Together Publications is committed to providing tried, trusted, and proven books that will further equip local churches to carry out the Great Commission. Your comments and suggestions are valued.

As each story develops, we offer possibilities of daily routines and feelings for each character based on the context of Scripture. These contextual illustrations are used to support the theme of the lesson and are not taken directly from Scripture.

Striving Together Publications
4020 E. Lancaster Blvd.
Lancaster, CA 93535
800.201.7748

Written by Joanne Bass
Cover design by Andrew Hutchens
Layout by Beth Lee
Layout design by Craig Parker
Contributors:

Terrie Chappell   Billy Willis
Danielle Mordh   Taniia Hymer
Tim Christoson   Alyssa Lofgren

ISBN 978–1-59894–186–9
Printed in the United States of America

Contents

How to Use This Curriculum

A Series of Thirteen Lessons

This curriculum series, *The Steps of Our Saviour*, focuses on thirteen events that occurred early in Jesus' earthly ministry. Each lesson contains a riveting story and emphasizes an applicable truth for children. Lessons are thoroughly supplemented with biblical references, teaching resources, and creative ideas.

The Life of Christ

This series is part of a larger, four-quarter, fifty-two lesson series on the life of Christ. The other three series include *The Signs of Our Saviour*, which focuses on our Lord's miracles; *The Stories of Our Saviour*, which focuses on our Lord's parables, and *The Sacrifice of Our Saviour*, which focuses on the betrayal, crucifixion, resurrection, and ascension of Christ.

Class Time

Each lesson contains sufficient resources to fill a ninety minute class period. For those attempting to use the curriculum for a sixty minute class period, we suggest the teacher choose which resources would be most effective and use them accordingly.

Age Appropriateness

This curriculum and its accompanying resources have been written for use with elementary-age children. Those who teach preschool-age children will also find it compatible for use with ages four and under.

Ideas & Resources Included

Experts suggest that we can estimate the average child's attention span as one minute per year of life. So for example, those teaching eight-year-olds should expect to change activities in the classroom every eight minutes or so, in order to keep the students' attention. The one exception to this rule would be the main Bible lesson itself. During the Bible lesson, attention can be kept through the combined use of visual aids such as flash cards, objects, role-play, digital projection, and a chalk/dry-erase board.

Included in Every Lesson:

One-Page Lesson Snapshot

At the beginning of each lesson is a summary page, intended to be photocopied by the teacher and tucked into his or her Bible for ready reference. This page may also be distributed to the assistant teachers in advance, so they may prepare for their classroom responsibilities. This page includes each week's lesson title, Scripture references, memory verse, lesson outline, and a suggested class schedule.

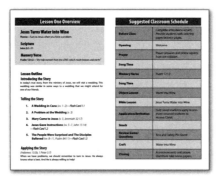

Scripture Passage

Great teaching begins with God's Word! Teachers should study the included Scripture passage numerous times throughout the week, make notes, and become familiar with the passage.

Teacher's Checklist

Use the weekly checklist to gather the appropriate materials in preparation for Sunday. Instructions may be given to an assistant teacher to pick up the needed items for the suggested craft, snack, game, or object lesson. The checklist identifies additional items found on the Ministry Resource CD (sold separately).

Snack Suggestion

Children will enjoy a different snack each week, which will not only be a treat but also a reminder of the truth learned. This is a fun and tasty way to give children a break during their time in the classroom.

Lesson Introduction

As each week's lesson begins, thought-provoking questions are asked, as students consider their own real-life circumstances, similar to those they will encounter in the Scripture. As you enter the lesson, allow for a brief period of answers and open discussion.

Verse-by-Verse Bible Lesson

Each lesson surveys a select portion of Scripture, taking a walk of discovery through the biblical record. Lessons are divided into five easy-to-identify points with helpful cross-references included.

Lesson Application

At the conclusion of each lesson, the teacher should seek to remind students of one or two primary truths to take away from the story. Then ask, in practical terms, how children might apply those truths during the week. At this time in the lesson, students who would like to receive Christ as Saviour should be encouraged to speak to a trained counselor.

Review Game with Questions

A unique theme-oriented game is included in each lesson for the purpose of review. While other questions may be added by the teacher, a list of initial review questions designed to reinforce the lesson are provided for use during the game.

Teaching the Memory Verse

A creative way of teaching the week's memory verse is included in each lesson. The Visual Resource Packet (sold separately) includes visuals for use with each memory verse. These visuals are also available on the Ministry Resource CD (sold separately).

Object Lesson

Children will remember the five-minute object lessons designed to support the Bible lesson. Each object lesson is easy to teach and simple to prepare using objects most of us have at home or that are available at a retail store.

Craft

Each lesson includes a craft that students and parents will enjoy putting on display! The craft section includes a supply list, easy-to-follow directions, and simple thoughts on how it relates to the Bible lesson.

Teaching Tips

Creative ideas and suggestions are provided for the purpose of effectively delivering the truths contained in each week's lesson.

Teacher's Note

Historical notes, practical instructions, and biblical definitions are provided to assist the teacher in study and preparation.

Suggested Visual Aids:

The "mixing up" of the weekly visuals will keep students engaged and will prevent predictability.

Flash Cards

In the thirteen lessons, flash cards are used to illustrate the Bible story (three cards for each selected story). Find the icon in the lesson margin to show the flash card to the students at the appropriate time. These twelve flash cards are included in the Visual Resource Packet (sold separately).

Act It Out

In certain lessons, we suggest selecting students to help "act out" the Bible story. Vary your choices in order to give all students who wish to be involved the opportunity to do so throughout the course of the series. The students more eager to participate in this role play are likely those who will benefit most from the exercise.

The Ministry Resource CD:

We recommend that each church or class purchase the Ministry Resource CD and make the files available to as many teachers as desired. This enables the investment in the CD to be spread over an unlimited volume and time.

Coloring Pages

Younger children (roughly three-year-olds through 3rd grade) will enjoy coloring a scene from each week's Bible lesson. Share an original copy with each teacher and provide as many photocopies as needed for all classes, one per student.

Activity Pages

Older children (roughly 3rd through 6th grades) will enjoy creative activities related to each week's Bible lesson. Activities include word searches, crossword puzzles, mazes, and brainteasers. Share an original copy with each teacher and provide as many photocopies as needed for all classes, one per student.

Student Take-Home Paper

The take-home paper is designed to help students take the Bible truth into the week ahead as they leave the classroom. Take-home papers will remind students of the weekly memory verse, include additional review questions, and suggest practical ways for applying the lesson in everyday experiences.

Share an original copy with each teacher and provide as many photocopies as needed for all classes, one per student.

PowerPoint Presentation

A Microsoft PowerPoint presentation is available for each of the thirteen lessons. If you have a television, computer monitor, or projector available, children will enjoy being able to follow the main points of the lesson on the screen. Each week's memory verse is also included in the presentation. These presentations are fully editable, and may be shared with as many teachers as desired. Feel free to move the PowerPoint files from the CD to your own computer, and to add or edit slides as you wish.

Memory Verse Visuals

The same visuals included in the Visual Resource Packet are included in PDF form on the Ministry Resource CD. These are provided so that teachers may use the images in projection or another form, including providing copies to students.

Craft and Game Templates

Throughout the series, templates are utilized with select crafts and games. These templates are found on the Ministry Resource CD in PDF form.

Suggested Classroom Schedule

Before Class	Complete attendance record. Provide students with coloring pages/activity pages.
Opening	Welcome
Prayer	Prayer requests and praise reports from the children
Song Time	
Memory Verse	John 3:30
Song Time	
Object Lesson	Bee with a Purpose
Bible Lesson	Jesus' Cousin is Born
Application/Invitation	Help saved students apply lesson. Invite unsaved students to receive Christ.
Snack	Thumbprint Cookie
Review Game/ Questions	Target Practice
Craft	Christmas Ornament
Closing	Give announcements and pray. Distribute take-home papers.

Lesson One Overview

Jesus' Cousin is Born

Theme—God has a purpose for your life.

Scripture
Luke 1:5–16, 57–58

Memory Verse
John 3:30—*"He must increase, but I must decrease."*

Lesson Outline
Introducing the Story
In today's story, we learn that God was going to bless Zacharias and Elisabeth by sending a special child into their lives. They were told the son that God would give them was going to grow up and become a mighty preacher to the people in Israel.

Telling the Story
1. Israel Is under Roman Rule *(v. 1)*

2. Zacharias and Elisabeth Obeyed the Laws of God and Man *(v. 6, Romans 13:1–2a, Acts 5:29)*

3. Elisabeth Was Barren *(v. 7, 1 Timothy 6:6)*

4. An Angel Comes to Zacharias *(vv. 11–16)—Flash Card 1.1*

5. John the Baptist Is Born *(vv. 57–58, 2 Timothy 2:13a)—Flash Card 1.2*

6. John Grows Up *(v. 80)—Flash Card 1.3*

Applying the Story
God created you with talents and characteristics to serve Him. He has a purpose for you just like He did for John, and you will enjoy following Him into your future.

1 Lesson One

Jesus' Cousin Is Born

Theme: God has a purpose for your life.

Scripture

Memory Verse

John 3:30
"He must increase, but I must decrease."

Luke 1:5–16, 57–58

5   There was in the days of Herod, the king of Judaea, a certain priest named Zacharias, of the course of Abia: and his wife was of the daughters of Aaron, and her name was Elisabeth.

6   And they were both righteous before God, walking in all the commandments and ordinances of the Lord blameless.

7   And they had no child, because that Elisabeth was barren, and they both were now well stricken in years.

8   And it came to pass, that while he executed the priest's office before God in the order of his course,

9   According to the custom of the priest's office, his lot was to burn incense when he went into the temple of the Lord.

10 And the whole multitude of the people were praying without at the time of incense.

11 And there appeared unto him an angel of the Lord standing on the right side of the altar of incense.

12 And when Zacharias saw him, he was troubled, and fear fell upon him.

13 But the angel said unto him, Fear not, Zacharias: for thy prayer is heard; and thy wife Elisabeth shall bear thee a son, and thou shalt call his name John.

14 And thou shalt have joy and gladness; and many shall rejoice at his birth.

15 For he shall be great in the sight of the Lord, and shall drink neither wine nor strong drink; and he shall be filled with the Holy Ghost, even from his mother's womb.

16 And many of the children of Israel shall he turn to the Lord their God.

57 Now Elisabeth's full time came that she should be delivered; and she brought forth a son.

58 And her neighbours and her cousins heard how the Lord had shewed great mercy upon her; and they rejoiced with her.

Teacher's Checklist

❑ Read Luke 1:5–16, 57–58 daily.

❑ Study Lesson One.

❑ Flash cards 1.1–1.3

❑ Prepare snack—Thumbprint Cookies.

❑ Gather for object lesson—picture of bees, honey.

❑ Gather for game—balloons, masking tape.

❑ Memory verse flash cards for John 3:30 (5 flash cards).

❑ Gather for craft—card stock, picture of student, ribbon.

❑ Print for craft—Christmas card ornament located on the resource CD.

❑ Print and duplicate Coloring Pages or Activity Pages on the Ministry Resource CD (one per student).

❑ Print and duplicate the Take-Home Paper on the Ministry Resource CD (one per student).

Snack Suggestion

Thumbprint Cookie
2/3 cup butter, softened
1/2 cup sugar
1 egg
1 teaspoon vanilla extract
1/4 teaspoon salt
1 2/3 cup flour

1. Cream the butter in a large bowl, gradually adding sugar, egg, and vanilla. Mix well.

2. Add salt and flour. Stir enough to form the dough. Cover and chill the dough for at least one hour.

3. Preheat oven to 375°. Make small balls, and set on a lightly greased baking sheet. Make an indent in the center of each ball with your thumb. Bake until golden brown, approximately 10 minutes.

Let the kids choose the topping for their cookie. Toppings: variety of jellies, marshmallow cream, and chocolate Nutella

Jesus has made each child with a specific purpose!

Bible Lesson

Scripture: Luke 1:5–16, 57–58

INTRODUCING THE STORY

Have you ever thought about what you want to be when you grow up? Some boys want to follow in the profession of their dads; or they dream of being a doctor, a famous actor, or the President of the United States. Many girls want to do what their mothers do—teach school, study law, or be a wife and mother.

What do you think you would like to do when you are grown? (Teacher, allow time for your students to answer.) What would you have to do to prepare for the profession you would like to have? Would you need to go to college, be an apprentice to someone who has the job you would like, or can you just learn on the job? (Again, allow your students to answer and give suggestions, such as what type of education, preparation, etc. they would need for a particular profession.)

The child who was born in our Bible story today grew to have a very unique profession, and we will see the special way God prepared him for his job.

Teacher's Note

Apprentice: a person who works for another in order to learn a trade; An apprentice is a person who learns the skills of a specific career by receiving on-the-job training from someone who is already an expert; One bound by legal agreement to work for another for a specific amount of time in return for instruction in a trade, art, or business.

THE STORY

1. Israel Is under Roman Rule (v. 1)

Zacharias and Elisabeth were a happy young Jewish couple living in Israel about two thousand years ago. At the time of Zacharias and Elisabeth, Israel wasn't a free nation, like the United States is today. Israel was ruled by another government—the government of Rome. The Romans didn't love the true God of the Bible—they worshipped false gods. The Romans also worshipped their governor, Caesar, as if he were a god! The Jews (the people of Israel) were enslaved by Rome, and they had to obey the laws of Herod, the Roman king.

2. Zacharias and Elisabeth Obeyed the Laws of God and Man (v. 6)

Zacharias and Elisabeth were careful to obey the Roman laws.

Romans 13:1–2a

1   Let every soul be subject unto the higher powers. For there is
     no power but of God: the powers that be are ordained of God.

2 a   Whosoever therefore resisteth the power, resisteth the
      ordinance of God:

Zacharias and Elisabeth were especially careful to obey God's laws. They were so careful that the Bible says about them, "And they were both righteous before God, walking in all the commandments and ordinances of the Lord blameless" (Luke 1:6). Although they lived under rulers who were against Christianity, and although most of the people around them didn't love God, Zacharias and Elisabeth chose to follow the Lord. They knew God's laws were even more important than man's laws.

Acts 5:29

29   Then Peter and the other apostles answered and said, We
     ought to obey God rather than men.

3. Elisabeth Was Barren (v. 7)

Zacharias was a priest in the temple. This was a job given to him by God, and he was faithful to perform all the duties God gave to him.

Zacharias and Elisabeth lived a happy life, serving and loving God and loving each other. There was one thing they wished for that they didn't have, however, and that was a child.

Day after day, as Elisabeth went out to work in her garden, she would watch the neighbor children run and play, and she had a great longing in her heart to have children of her own.

Soon the days turned into weeks, and the weeks turned into years. Elisabeth continued to watch the neighbor children as she went about her daily housework. She got to know the children, and she became like an aunt to many of them. She read stories to them, baked treats for them, prayed for them, and hugged them often. But Elisabeth and her husband, Zacharias, "had no child, because that Elisabeth was barren" (Luke 1:7a).

Remember, Zacharias and Elisabeth loved God, and they trusted Him to always give them what was best. They continued to read God's Word, talk to Him in prayer, and obey Him. Zacharias faithfully served God as a priest, and Elisabeth faithfully served God as Zacharias' wife. Although they wished for a child, their lives were full of joy as they served God together.

1 Timothy 6:6

6 *But godliness with contentment is great gain.*

4. An Angel Comes to Zacharias (vv. 11–16)

Then, one day, when Zacharias and Elisabeth were too old to have children, their lives were changed forever in a miraculous way! Zacharias was away from home working in the temple. His job was to burn incense in the temple, and many people were outside praying. "And there appeared unto him an angel of the Lord standing on the right side of the altar of incense" (Luke 1:11).

Zacharias had never seen an angel before, and he became full of fear. The angel spoke to Zacharias, "Don't be afraid, Zacharias. I am here for a very special purpose. God has heard your prayers as you have asked Him to give you a child of your own, and now Elisabeth will have a son, and you will name him John."

The angel went on to say, "He is going to give you joy and gladness, and many other people will rejoice when he is born as well. He is going to be a very special man. God already has his life all planned out. You will need to train him just as God says. He is going to be a prophet, telling people to be ready for the Saviour who is coming, and many people will turn to the Saviour because of your son's message."

Imagine: Zacharias and Elisabeth were too old to have children, and now an angel is telling Zacharias that his wife is going to have a baby. The angel is not only telling Zacharias that his wife is going to have a baby, but he is telling Zacharias that God already has the baby's life all planned—and he hasn't even been born yet!

Teacher's Note

Barren: unable to bear children

Flash Card 1.1

Teaching Tip

Zacharias was a descendant of Aaron, the priest. Only descendants of Aaron were allowed by God to be priests. Elisabeth was a descendant of Aaron, as well.

Zacharias could hardly believe what the angel said! "I am an old man, and my wife well stricken in years," (Luke 1:18). Zacharias said to the angel. "We're too old to have children!"

Flash Card 1.2

Teacher's Note

Faithful: true; worthy of belief

5. John the Baptist Is Born (vv. 57–58)

But several months later, just as the angel had said, Elisabeth gave birth to a son. "And her neighbours and her cousins heard how the Lord had shewed great mercy upon her; and they rejoiced with her" (Luke 1:58). It was just as God had promised through the angel! Elisabeth, who was too old to give birth to a child, had a son, and they named him John. (We call him John the Baptist.) And, just as the angel had said, many other people rejoiced with her when her son was born. God always keeps His Word.

2 Timothy 2:13a

13a If we believe not, yet he abideth faithful:

Flash Card 1.3

6. John Grows Up (v. 80)

As John grew up, Zacharias and Elisabeth believed God and followed His plan for John as they trained him. They knew God had a very special purpose for John's life, and his parents wanted him to be able to fulfill it exactly as God had planned. "And the child grew, and waxed strong in spirit" (Luke 1: 80a).

God knew something very special when He told Zacharias that Elisabeth was going to have a baby. God knew that Elisabeth's cousin, Mary, was going to give birth to Jesus, the Saviour, about six months after John would be born. God planned for John to be the very special preacher who would tell the people that the Saviour for whom they had been waiting was finally here, and that they needed to trust in Him.

There had been many prophets in the Old Testament who told about the coming Messiah—Isaiah, Micah, and Hosea were some of those prophets. There were others as well, and they were all sent by God to tell of Jesus Christ. But John was going to be the last prophet to point the way to the Saviour. Jesus would already be living on earth when John was prophesying about Him—John had the very important job of being the very last prophet to tell of the coming Messiah who would deliver from sin anyone who trusted in Him.

And John did exactly what God had planned for him. When he was grown, John spent his life telling people about the Saviour, preparing them to receive and trust in Him. Some people believed John the Baptist's words about the Saviour, and some didn't; but John kept on telling everyone, because that was the job God gave him to do.

Teaching Tip

Jesus: Saviour or Deliverer

Messiah: (Hebrew) Anointed One, one set apart for special duties

Christ: Greek word for "Messiah"

APPLYING THE STORY

It is easy to see that John the Baptist was a very special person. Before John was even born, God had his whole life planned out. And the plan God had for John's life was amazing!

What if John had chosen a different job than the one God had planned for him? What if John hadn't spent his life telling people about the Saviour? Who would have done what God created John to do?

John could have chosen his own way. John could have ignored what God wanted for him, and he could have done what he wanted instead. But John wouldn't have been happy if he had chosen not to follow God's plan for him. God created each of us with a specific purpose, and we will be happiest when we are fulfilling that purpose.

Do you know you are a very special person, just like John the Baptist? Just as God had a plan for John's life, He has a plan for your life. Just as God knew exactly what He wanted John to do before he was even born, God knew exactly what He wanted you to do before you were even born. And, like John's, the plan God has for your life is amazing!

Psalm 100:3a

3a   Know ye that the LORD he is God: it is he that hath made us, and not we ourselves;

Psalm 139:16

16   Thine eyes did see my substance, yet being unperfect; and in thy book all my members were written, which in continuance were fashioned, when as yet there was none of them.

Jeremiah 29:11

11 *For I know the thoughts that I think toward you, saith the LORD, thoughts of peace, and not of evil, to give you an expected end.*

Although God knows what job He has for you when you grow up, most of you don't know yet what that job is.

- Maybe He wants you to be a preacher like John, telling people about Jesus.
- Maybe He wants you to be a farmer, providing food for other people.
- Maybe He wants you to be a doctor or nurse, helping sick people get well.
- Maybe He wants you to be a teacher, training children or adults for the jobs He has for them.
- Maybe He wants you to be a Sunday school teacher, helping others know the Bible.
- Maybe He wants you to be a carpenter, building houses to give people shelter.
- Maybe He wants you to be a mother who stays at home, training your children.
- Maybe He wants you to be a lawyer, a plumber, a secretary, a road construction worker, or an electrician.
- There are many jobs in the world, and God has one planned just for you!

How can you be sure that you find just the right plan and purpose God has for you? You can find God's special plan for your future by following the plan He has for you right now. He gives instructions in the Bible, and when we follow them, we are on the right path for finding His exact plan for our whole lives.

God wants every person to trust Jesus as his Saviour. If a person doesn't know Jesus as his Saviour, he will never know God's plan for him.

2 Peter 3:9

9 *The Lord is…not willing that any should perish, but that all should come to repentance.*

The Steps of Our Saviour | © 2011 Striving Together Publications

God wants every person to read the Bible every day. He uses His Word to show us what He wants us to do and where He wants us to go. His Word is full of instructions to show us His plan for each day of our lives.

Teaching Note

This would be an ideal time to share the plan of salvation with your students.

Psalm 119:105

105   Thy word is a lamp unto my feet, and a light unto my path.

God wants every person to talk to Him in prayer.

Psalm 62:8a

8a   Trust in him at all times; ye people, pour out your heart before him:

God wants every child to obey his or her parents.

Ephesians 6:1

1   Children obey your parents in the Lord, for this is right.

God wants every person to obey the laws of the government.

Titus 3:1

1   Put them in mind to be subject to principalities and powers, to obey magistrates, to be ready to every good work

God wants every Christian to tell others about the Saviour.

Mark 16:15

15   And he said unto them, Go ye into all the world, and preach the gospel to every creature.

When you follow God's plan for your life now—the plan He shows you in the Bible—you will be on the path toward following His special plan—the one He prepared just for you—for the rest of your life. Then, just like John the Baptist, you can fulfill the exact purpose for which God created you.

Review Game/Questions

Target Practice

Materials needed
- Small balloons
- Masking tape

Set up

Before class mark the floor with masking tape into a box shaped target. The bulls eye is worth 100 points, the second square 50 points and the outer square 25 points.

Playing the Game

Divide the class into two teams. Ask Team 1 a review question. If the student answers correctly he can blow up his balloon, but rather than tie the neck in a knot, let the balloon go. Note where the balloon lands according to the target and give the team those points. Repeat with Team 2. The team with the most points after all the questions are answered wins.

Diagram:

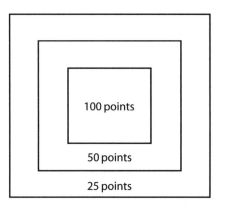

1. What nation ruled Israel at the time when Zacharias and Elisabeth were living?
    Answer: Rome

2. How did Zacharias and Elisabeth treat the law of God?
    Answer: They were careful to obey it.

3. What was the one thing Zacharias and Elisabeth wished for that they didn't have?
    Answer: A child

4. Who visited Zacharias in the temple?
    Answer: An angel

5. What emotion did Zacharias feel when he saw the angel?
    Answer: He was full of fear.

6. What promise did the angel give to Zacharias?
    Answer: Zacharias and Elisabeth would have a son.

7. How did Zacharias respond to the angel's announcement?
    Answer: He could not believe it because Elisabeth was too old to have children.

8. What did Zacharias and Elisabeth name the baby? What do we call him today?
    Answer: John, John the Baptist

9. What was God's special plan for John?
    Answer: He told everyone about Jesus and prepared them to receive Him.

10. What are some things God has planned for us to do right now?
    Answer: Answers will vary, but may include: praying, attending church, obeying our parents, and being kind to others.

Teaching the Memory Verse

John 3:30

30   He must increase, but I must decrease.

Begin talking about yourself. "I can do this" and "I can do that! I can do it by myself!" Then add that you love Jesus, too. After a minute or two, ask, "What is wrong with my attitude?" I have made myself more important than my relationship with Jesus. God has a plan for our lives and we cannot do it all by ourselves. We need Jesus! Our attitudes and our actions should be for Him to increase and for us to decrease. Christ must take preeminence in our lives and not us. As we grow in our faith, Christ must be seen and not us.

Print the visuals for John 3:30. Show the class flash card #1. Have the class read the verse from the flash card. Show the class flash card #2. Have the class read the verse from the flash card. Showing flash card #3 say, "Let's read the verse again. The words are getting smaller, but I think you can still read it." Continue in this fashion with flash cards #4 and #5. Now tell the class, "I think we can say the verse without any help at all!" Let the students say the verse without the flash cards.

Variation: As the students say the verse, have them say "He must increase" in a loud voice and "but I must decrease" in a quiet voice. For each flash card, the class can increase the volume when saying "He must increase" and get softer when saying "but I must decrease."

Object Lesson—Bee with a Purpose

Bring a bee in a jar, or a picture of a bee. You can even bring honey and allow the children to taste it. Say:

Many of us believe bees really do not have that great of a purpose. When a bee flies close to us, we see them only as a pest that may sting us. However, bees were born with a purpose greater than stinging people! They also do more than make the honey we like to put on biscuits! Bees actually cross-pollinate our flowers, and are greatly responsible for the fruit and vegetables we have to eat. A bee is constantly working for a purpose. **It was born to serve**. It knows nothing else.

If a simple honey bee was created for the purpose to serve, don't you think you were born with a much greater purpose? The difference is that a bee never questions its purpose; it just serves. You, however, can question your purpose and refuse to serve the Lord. If bees are responsible for something as important as the food we eat, then you have an even greater purpose.

Facts about the honey bee:

Honeybees use nectar to make honey. Nectar is almost 80% water with some complex sugars. In fact, if you have ever pulled a honeysuckle blossom out of its stem, nectar is the clear liquid that drops from the end of the blossom. In North America, bees get nectar from flowers like clovers, dandelions, berry bushes, and fruit tree blossoms. They use their long, tubelike tongues like straws to suck the nectar out of the flowers, and they store it in their "honey stomachs."

Bees actually have two stomachs—their honey stomach which they use like a nectar backpack, and their regular stomach. The honey stomach holds almost 70 milligrams of nectar when full, and it weighs almost as much as the bee does. Honeybees must visit between 100 and 1,500 flowers in order to fill their honey stomachs.

The honeybees return to the hive and pass the nectar on to other worker bees. These "house bees" suck the nectar from the honeybee's stomach through their mouths, and chew the nectar for about half an hour. During this time, enzymes are breaking the complex sugars in the nectar into simple sugars so that it is both more digestible for the bees and less likely to be attacked by bacteria while it is stored within the hive. The bees then spread the nectar throughout the honeycombs where water evaporates from it, making it a thicker syrup. The bees make the nectar dry even faster by fanning it with their wings. Once the honey is gooey enough, the bees seal off the cell of the honeycomb with a plug of wax. The honey is stored until it is eaten. In one year, a colony of bees eats between 120 and 200 pounds of honey.

Craft—Christmas Ornament

Getting It Together

Card stock
Camera
Printer
Ribbon
Christmas Ornament pattern from the Ministry Resource CD

Putting It Together

1. Print out a Christmas ornament for each student on card stock.
2. Take a photo of each student, and print the photo.
3. Have each student glue the photo onto the decorated paper.

Seeing It Together

God has made each student with a specific purpose. As each student glues their photo to the paper, remind them how much God loves them and created them for a special purpose.

Additional Resources

Find the following items on the Ministry Resource CD:

• Coloring Page (for younger children)

• Activity Page (for older children)

• Student Take-Home Paper

• PowerPoint Presentation

Suggested Classroom Schedule

Before Class	Complete attendance record. Provide students with coloring pages/activity pages.
Opening	Welcome
Prayer	Prayer requests and praise reports from the children
Song Time	
Memory Verse	Psalm 118:6
Song Time	
Object Lesson	Family Tree
Bible Lesson	An Angel Visits Mary and Joseph
Application/Invitation	Help saved students apply lesson. Invite unsaved students to receive Christ.
Snack	Christmas Snack Mix
Review Game/ Questions	Goody Gumdrop
Craft	Candy Cane Ornament
Closing	Give announcements and pray. Distribute take-home papers.

Lesson Two Overview

An Angel Visits Mary and Joseph

Theme—Don't fear God's plan for your life.

Scriptures

Luke 1:26–38, Matthew 1:18–21

Memory Verse

Psalm 118:6—"The LORD is on my side; I will not fear: what can man do unto me?"

Lesson Outline

Introducing the Story

Today's story introduces us to Mary and Joseph. Let's learn how God helped them overcome their fear as He shared His plan with them.

Telling the Story

1. **Mary's Engagement** (Luke 1:26–27, Genesis 3:15, Romans 6:23a, Revelation 20:14–15)—Flash Card 2.1

2. **The Angel Gabriel's Message to Mary** (vv. 26–37, Isaiah 7:14)—Flash Card 2.2

3. **Mary's Response to the Angel's News** (v. 38, Psalm 119:68a, Jeremiah 31:3b, 29:11, Psalm 56:3)

4. **Joseph's Response to Mary's News** (Matthew 1:18–19)

5. **Joseph's Dream** (vv. 20–23)—Flash Card 2.3

6. **Joseph's Response** (vv. 24–25)

Applying the Story

God wants us to respond in faith and follow Him instead of fearing our circumstances. There's no need to fear God's plan for our lives!

2 Lesson Two

An Angel Visits Mary and Joseph

Theme: Don't fear God's plan for your life.

Scriptures

Luke 1:26–38

26 *And in the sixth month the angel Gabriel was sent from God unto a city of Galilee, named Nazareth,*

27 *To a virgin espoused to a man whose name was Joseph, of the house of David; and the virgin's name was Mary.*

28 *And the angel came in unto her, and said, Hail, thou that art highly favoured, the Lord is with thee: blessed art thou among women.*

29 *And when she saw him, she was troubled at his saying, and cast in her mind what manner of salutation this should be.*

30 *And the angel said unto her, Fear not, Mary: for thou hast found favour with God.*

31 *And, behold, thou shalt conceive in thy womb, and bring forth a son, and shalt call his name JESUS.*

32 *He shall be great, and shall be called the Son of the Highest: and the Lord God shall give unto him the throne of his father David:*

33 *And he shall reign over the house of Jacob for ever; and of his kingdom there shall be no end.*

34 *Then said Mary unto the angel, How shall this be, seeing I know not a man?*

35 *And the angel answered and said unto her, The Holy Ghost shall come upon thee, and the power of the Highest shall overshadow thee: therefore also that holy thing which shall be born of thee shall be called the Son of God.*

36 *And, behold, thy cousin Elisabeth, she hath also conceived a son in her old age: and this is the sixth month with her, who was called barren.*

37 *For with God nothing shall be impossible.*

38 *And Mary said, Behold the handmaid of the Lord; be it unto me according to thy word. And the angel departed from her.*

Matthew 1:18–21

18 *Now the birth of Jesus Christ was on this wise: When as his mother Mary was espoused to Joseph, before they came together, she was found with child of the Holy Ghost.*

19 *Then Joseph her husband, being a just man, and not willing to make her a publick example, was minded to put her away privily.*

20 *But while he thought on these things, behold, the angel of the Lord appeared unto him in a dream, saying, Joseph, thou son of David, fear not to take unto thee Mary thy wife: for that which is conceived in her is of the Holy Ghost.*

21 *And she shall bring forth a son, and thou shalt call his name JESUS: for he shall save his people from their sins.*

Teacher's Checklist

☐ Read Luke 1:26–38 and Matthew 1:18–21 daily.

☐ Study Lesson Two.

☐ Flash cards 2.1–2.3

☐ Prepare snack—Bugles, Pretzels, M&M's, and Hershey Kisses.

☐ Gather for object lesson—Copy of a family tree.

☐ Gather for game—Gumdrop pattern located on the Ministry Resource CD, gift bag, pocket chart, or magnets.

☐ Memory verse flash cards for Psalm 118:6 (3 cards).

☐ Purchase for craft—candy canes, wooden circles, fabric, pen, glue, and raffia.

☐ Print and duplicate Coloring Pages or Activity Pages on the Ministry Resource CD (one per student).

☐ Print and duplicate the Take-Home Paper on the Ministry Resource CD (one per student).

Snack Suggestion

Christmas Snack Mix

Bugles Corn Snacks— Shaped like a trumpet to remind us of the angel who proclaimed the birth of Jesus

Pretzels—Hands folded in prayer; Joseph who prayed and obeyed God

M&Ms—Mary who said "Be it unto me according to your will"

Hershey's Kisses—The love of Jesus who was born for us

Bible Lesson

Scripture: Luke 1:26–38, Matthew 1:18–21

INTRODUCING THE STORY

What scares you the most—what are you afraid of? A quality that many fears have in common is that the person with the fear doesn't have a good understanding of what frightens them.

Many children are afraid of the dark. After they are in bed and the lights are turned off, they start thinking about what might possibly be there that they can't see. They think of all kinds of scary things, and they lie there awake and afraid of something they don't understand. If someone would just turn on the light, in most cases the child would see that everything is just as it was when the light was turned off. There are no wild animals, prowlers, or monsters. They had nothing to fear.

Last week we learned about the special plan God had for John the Baptist—he was to be the last prophet to tell the world about the coming Saviour. In fact, John had the privilege of telling people that the Saviour from sin for which they were waiting was already here! We also learned that God has a special plan for your life, as well.

This week we are going to learn about two other people and the special plans God had for their lives. We will see that God's plan for our lives is something we never need to fear, no matter how different it may be than our own plans.

THE STORY

1. Mary's Engagement (Luke 1:26–27)

Mary was a young Jewish woman living in Nazareth, a city of Galilee, about two thousand years ago. There was something very special about Mary— she loved God with all her heart.

In Mary's time, all the Jewish people were waiting for a Saviour to come to save them from their sins. Way back in the Garden of Eden, right after Adam and Eve sinned for the first time, God promised that He would send a Saviour to save everyone who trusts in Him from Satan, sin, and death.

Teaching Tip

Allow time for students to express their fears. To add interest and fun, you could even find the names of some common fears and have that list with you at class so you can share with your students the name of the fear they experience. Some examples are:

ligyrophobia: fear of loud noises
ornithophobia: fear of birds

As children mention their fears, remember that even some of these simple fears (including fear of the dark) are well-grounded in the child's mind. Be careful not to ridicule their fears, but rather, encourage them throughout this lesson to trust God.

Flash Card 2.1

Genesis 3:15

15 *And I will put enmity between thee and the woman, and between thy seed and her seed; it shall bruise thy head, and thou shalt bruise his heel.*

Mary believed God, and every day she wondered, "Is this the day God is going to send the Messiah to us?" Mary, like all the Jewish girls and women of her day, hoped that somehow she would be the one chosen to give birth to the Messiah—the Saviour. Mary knew that she, like all of us, was a sinner, and she knew she needed a Saviour to save her from her sin and from the punishment of sin, which is death.

Romans 6:23a

23a *For the wages of sin is death;*

Revelation 20:14–15

14 *And death and hell were cast into the lake of fire. This is the second death.*

15 *And whosoever was not found written in the book of life was cast into the lake of fire.*

Every day, as Mary read her Bible, she looked forward to the coming Messiah. Every day she prayed to God. Oh, Mary did other things, as well. She sewed and sang and took care of children. She went for walks in the sunshine, cleaned her family's home, and cooked meals. She did all the things young women of her day did, but she did them with the joy of God in her heart, because she knew Him through His Word, and she trusted Him.

Then, one day, a day for which Mary had been preparing her whole life, finally came. No, it wasn't that God had sent the Messiah—not yet, anyway. This day to which she had been looking forward for so long was her engagement. A young man who loved God with all his heart, just like Mary did, asked Mary to be his wife. They were going to be married!

Mary was full of plans and hopes and dreams. They would get married and have a little house of their own. She would cook and sew and clean for Joseph. All the things she had been learning to do as a daughter in her parents' home, she would now do for Joseph—as his wife! They would have children and raise them for the Lord. The whole world looked bright and happy to Mary as she became engaged to Joseph.

2. The Angel Gabriel's Message to Mary (vv. 26–37)

Flash Card 2.2

Not long after their engagement, Mary had an experience that changed her life forever. God sent His angel Gabriel to Mary with a message. The angel said, "Mary, God is with you, and you have found great favor with Him. You are going to be honored by God more than any other woman."

"And when she saw him, she was troubled at his saying," (Luke 1:29a). Mary wondered, "Why would an angel be talking to me? I am just a poor Jewish girl—why would God send His angel to me? Why would he speak so highly of me?"

The angel said, "Don't be afraid. You have found favor with God. You, Mary, are the one God has chosen to be the mother of the promised Saviour. You, Mary, will 'bring forth a son, and shalt call his name JESUS' (Luke 1:31b). "The son to whom you give birth will be great—He will be the Son of God!"

Mary had read her Bible, and she knew God's promise in the Old Testament.

Isaiah 7:14

14 *Therefore the Lord himself shall give you a sign: Behold a virgin shall conceive, and bear a son, and shall call his name Immanuel.*

She knew that the mother of the Saviour would be a virgin. But now, when the angel was telling her that she would be the mother of the Saviour, she wondered how it could really be. She knew that for a virgin, as she was, to have a child was impossible according to the laws of nature. So she said to the angel Gabriel, "How shall this be, seeing I know not a man?" (Luke 1:34).

The angel told Mary that she was right. It would be impossible unless God did a miracle. And that is exactly what God was going to do. The angel said that the Holy Spirit would place the baby in Mary's womb, and that the child to whom she would give birth would be the very Son of God. Mary would be His mother, but God would be His Father!

The angel continued, "Your cousin Elisabeth, who is very old—much too old to give birth to a child—is going to have a child, too. Her baby is going to be born in three months." It would also be impossible for Elisabeth to have a child, unless God did a miracle, and that is just what He did. "For with God nothing shall be impossible" (Luke 1:37).

Teacher's Note

Explain to students that the womb is the Bible word for "a mommy's stomach."

3. Mary's Response to the Angel's News (v. 38)

As the angel stood there, Mary thought about the amazing things he had just told her. Then, her thoughts turned to the people she knew. She wouldn't be honored by them, as the angel had told her she would be honored by God. People—her friends and relatives—would think she had sinned against God, having a baby when she wasn't even married yet. She thought of Joseph, whom she loved so dearly—would Joseph believe her when she told him that she had kept her promise of faithfulness to him, and that the baby to whom she was going to give birth was actually the Son of God? How would she ever tell Joseph?! It was a fearful thing to think of being misunderstood by everyone she knew and loved. What would happen to her life? Would she lose her opportunity to marry the man she loved, and would everyone think of her as a sinful woman from now on?

But then Mary's thoughts turned to God. Mary knew God through His Word. She knew that God was good.

Psalm 119:68a

68a Thou art good, and doest good

Mary knew that God loved her and had good plans for her.

Jeremiah 31:3b

3b Yea, I have loved thee with an everlasting love

Jeremiah 29:11

11 For I know the thoughts that I think toward you, saith the LORD, thoughts of peace, and not of evil, to give you an expected end.

Mary knew she could trust God with her life. The angel had said she was to be honored by God—honored above all women. No other woman in the world was ever going to be able to give birth to the Saviour, for there would only be one Saviour. God was finally going to send the promised Saviour, and He was going to use her to give birth to Him. Her son would be great, and He would be the Son of God!

Yes, Mary knew God's plan for her was better than her own, and she would trust Him. She would trust Him, and not be afraid.

Psalm 56:3

3   *What time I am afraid, I will trust in thee.*

Mary looked at the angel and said, "Behold the handmaid of the Lord; be it unto me according to thy word" (Luke 1:38). "I am God's servant. I will do what you have said, just as God wants."

4. Joseph's Response to Mary's News (Matthew 1:18–19)

The time came that Joseph found out Mary was going to have a baby. Joseph knew that the child was not his, since he and Mary had not yet been together as husband and wife. Joseph was a good man, and he thought long and hard about what he should do.

"What does this mean?" Joseph wondered. "What has Mary done? I wonder what I should do? I truly love Mary, but we shouldn't get married now—her baby isn't mine. Oh, this is so painful. I know, I'll just quietly divorce her. No one needs to know. I don't want her reputation to be damaged. I'll just go on with my life, and she can go on with hers. This hurts me so much!"

Teacher's Note

Divorce was the procedure required for "putting away" in a betrothal relationship.

5. Joseph's Dream (vv. 20–23)

Flash Card 2.3

"But while he thought on these things, behold, the angel of the Lord appeared unto him in a dream, saying, Joseph, thou son of David, fear not to take unto thee Mary thy wife: for that which is conceived in her is of the Holy Ghost" (Matthew 1:20).

The angel told Joseph not to be afraid to take Mary as his wife, for the child to whom she was going to give birth was the Son of God. Mary didn't need to worry at all whether or not Joseph was going to understand. God took care of that for her—He told Joseph Himself!

Then, the angel told Joseph that when Mary's son was born, Joseph was to "call his name JESUS: for he shall save his people from their sins" (Matthew 1:21). Mary was going to be the mother of the Saviour, who would save from sin everyone who puts his trust in Him!

Teacher's Note

The name *Jesus* means "Jehovah the Saviour."

6. Joseph's Response (vv. 24–25)

Joseph may have had the same thoughts Mary had: "What will people think? Will this damage our reputations? Can I really trust God?"

But, the Bible says, "Then Joseph being raised from sleep did as the angel of the Lord had bidden him, and took unto him his wife" (Matthew 1:24). Like Mary, Joseph knew God through reading the Bible. Like Mary, Joseph knew that God loved him and that he could trust God to lead him in the right way and to take care of him. So, Joseph obediently did exactly what God told him to do: he took Mary as his wife, and when the baby was born, Joseph named Him Jesus.

APPLYING THE STORY

Mary and Joseph each heard the same two words from the angel: "Fear not." God knows it is very easy for people to be afraid. He knew that both Mary and Joseph were being asked by God to do things they didn't understand and that they would likely be afraid.

God knew something else. He knew that His plan for Mary and His plan for Joseph were the best plans in the world for them. He knew they would be happier fulfilling His plans for them than they would be doing anything else.

God also knew His plan for Mary and Joseph would be the best plan for the whole world, because His plan was to send the Saviour through Mary and to give her Joseph as her husband to protect her as she raised Jesus. And the whole world needed a Saviour.

God didn't only tell Mary and Joseph to fear not, to not be afraid. He has told us many times through His Word, the Bible, not to be afraid.

Deuteronomy 31:6

6   *Be strong and of a good courage, fear not, nor be afraid of them: for the LORD thy God, he it is that doth go with thee; he will not fail thee, nor forsake thee.*

Joshua 1:9

9   *Have not I commanded thee? Be strong and of a good courage; be not afraid, neither be thou dismayed: for the LORD thy God is with thee whithersoever thou goest.*

Psalm 56:11

11   *In God have I put my trust: I will not be afraid what man can do unto me.*

Isaiah 41:10

10   *Fear thou not; for I am with thee: be not dismayed; for I am thy God: I will strengthen thee; yea, I will help thee; yea, I will uphold thee with the right hand of my righteousness.*

Isaiah 41:13

13   *For I the LORD thy God will hold thy right hand, saying unto thee, Fear not; I will help thee.*

John 14:27b

27b   *Let not your heart be troubled, neither let it be afraid.*

God had a plan for Mary's life; He had a plan for Joseph's life; and He has a plan for your life. God's plan is the best possible plan for a life.

Sometimes the plan God reveals to us seems frightening. It is often filled with things we've never experienced and don't understand. We may not see how it can even work out right. But, just as Mary trusted God, and just as Joseph trusted God, we can trust God that His plan is good for our lives, too. Just as God told Mary and Joseph to "fear not," He tells each of us to "fear not."

When Mary heard God's plan for her, she yielded her heart to God and said, "Behold the handmaid of the Lord; be it unto me according to thy word." And, although she didn't understand how He would work it out, God led her step by step through His plan for her life. He will do that for you, too, if you yield your heart to His plan for you, trusting Him even when you are afraid and when you don't understand.

Joseph also yielded to God. When the angel told him to take Mary as his wife, he "did as the angel of the Lord had bidden him." And, although he didn't understand how God would work it out, God led him step by step through His plan for Joseph's life. He will do that for you, too, if you yield your heart to His plan for you, trusting Him when you are afraid and when you don't understand.

Teacher's Note

Yield: to surrender; to comply with; to submit; to give way; to not oppose

 **Review Game/Questions**

Goody Gumdrop

Materials needed
- Gumdrop pattern from the Ministry Resource CD
- Gift Bag
- Something to display gumdrops (e.g., pocket chart, flannel, magnet, etc.)

Set up

Print 40 gumdrops on two different colors of cardstock (e.g., 20 red and 20 green). Cut out the gumdrops (laminate for durability). If you want gumdrops to adhere to flannel board or white board, prepare the back of the gumdrop with Velcro or magnet strip. Put all the gumdrops in the gift bag.

Playing the Game

Divide the class into two teams. Each team corresponds with one of the colored gumdrops. Ask a student from the first team a question. If the student answers correctly, that student may (without looking) pick a gumdrop from the bag. The gumdrop goes, not necessarily to the student's team, but to the team with the same color. The object of the game is to see which team will have the most gumdrops of its color when the game is over. At the end of the game, give each student a real gumdrop to eat.

1. Who asked Mary to be his wife?
    Answer: Joseph

2. After Mary got engaged, who came to her with a message that would change her life forever?
    Answer: The angel, Gabriel

3. What did Mary feel when the angel came to her?
    Answer: She felt afraid.

4. What was the special message Gabriel gave to Mary?
    Answer: She would give birth to Jesus, the promised Saviour.

5. What did Mary say to the angel?
    Answer: "Be it unto me according to thy word."

6. What did Joseph consider doing when he found out Mary was having a baby?
    Answer: He was going to quietly break off their engagement.

7. What did the angel tell Joseph?
    Answer: Fear not. Mary will give birth to the Son of God.

8. What name was the baby to be given?
    Answer: The angel told Joseph to name the baby Jesus.

9. Did Joseph obey the angel?
    Answer: Yes

10. What can you do (as Mary and Joseph did) when you are afraid?
    Answer: Trust God and yield to (or obey) Him.

 # Teaching the Memory Verses

Psalm 118:6

*6   The LORD is on my side; I will not fear: what can man do
     unto me?*

Introduce the first flash card. Explain this is the reference. It lets us know where we can find this verse in the Bible. Invite a student to come hold flash card #1. Have students repeat the reference.

Call on another student to hold flash card #2. Tell the students that when we have Christ in our hearts, when we are saved, the Lord is on our side. He is with us all the time. Repeat flash card #1 and flash card #2.

Bring up another student to hold flash card #3. Talk with the students about fear. With the Lord on our side, we don't have to fear. It is a choice—"I will not fear." Have students recite all three flash cards.

Have one student hold the last flash card. Man cannot do anything to me that God doesn't allow. And, if God allows a circumstance to come our way, He is right there with us. We don't have to face it alone. That's a promise. Have the class say all four flash cards several times.

Visual Aid
Print the flash cards for Psalm 118:6. Laminate for durability.

Object Lesson—Family Tree

When the angels visited Mary and Joseph they were very specific on what family the Lord Jesus would come from. Jesus would come from the family of King David.

Family trees are often presented with the oldest generations at the top and the newer generations at the bottom. An ancestry chart, which is a tree showing the ancestors of an individual, will more closely resemble a tree in shape, being wider at the top than the bottom. In some ancestry charts, an individual appears on the left and his or her ancestors appear to the right. A descendancy chart, which depicts all the descendants of an individual, will be narrowest at the top.

So, God chose Mary, who came from the family of King David, to carry Jesus. Jesus was kin or in the same family as King David.

Jesus also calls us His sons and daughters. We are not of the direct lineage of Jesus, but we are "grafted" into the family. We are adopted into Jesus' family tree!

Cut a limb from another piece of paper and write your name on it and stick it to Jesus' family tree. We enter the family tree of Jesus by accepting Him as our Lord and Saviour.

 # Additional Resources

Find the following items on the Ministry Resource CD:

- Coloring Page (for younger children)
- Activity Page (for older children)
- Student Take-Home Paper
- PowerPoint Presentation

Craft—Candy Cane Ornament

Getting It Together

Candy cane—1 per student
Wooden circles
Fabric
Pen
Glue
Raffia

Putting It Together

1. Make a face on the circle.
2. Using fabric, glue clothes on the wooden circle, making a baby.
3. Glue the raffia and the baby onto the candy cane.

Seeing It Together

We don't have to fear God's plan for our life. As we follow God's Word, we can trust God's perfect plan for our lives.

Suggested Classroom Schedule

Before Class	Complete attendance record. Provide students with coloring pages/activity pages.
Opening	Welcome
Prayer	Prayer requests and praise reports from the children
Song Time	
Memory Verse	Luke 2:11
Song Time	
Object Lesson	Christmas Box
Bible Lesson	Jesus Is Born in Bethlehem
Application/Invitation	Help saved students apply lesson. Invite unsaved students to receive Christ.
Snack	Birthday Cake for Jesus
Review Game/ Questions	Christmas Card Review Game
Craft	Jesus Is Born Magnet
Closing	Give announcements and pray. Distribute take-home papers.

Lesson Three Overview

Jesus is Born in Bethlehem

Theme—The arrival of Jesus is the greatest of miracles.

Scripture
Luke 2:1–18

Memory Verse
Luke 2:11—"For unto you is born this day in the city of David a Saviour, which is Christ the Lord."

Lesson Outline

Introducing the Story (John 3:16)

There is one miracle that everyone who has ever lived needed God to do. That miracle was for all people, of all time, in every place in the world. Today we are going to learn about the greatest miracle of all time.

Telling the Story

1. **The Trip to Bethlehem** (vv. 1–5)—Flash Card 3.1
2. **The Birth of Jesus** (vv. 6–7, Micah 5:2, Matthew 2:5–6) —Flash Card 3.2
3. **The Shepherds Receive a Birth Announcement** (vv. 8–14) —Flash Card 3.3
4. **The Shepherds Go to See the Baby** (vv. 15–16)
5. **The Shepherds Share the Good News** (vv. 17–18)
6. **Mary Thinks About What Happened** (v. 19)
7. **The Shepherds Praise God** (v. 20)

Applying the Story (Genesis 3:15, John 3:16)

The miracle of Jesus' birth was for all people, in all places, for all time. All people are sinners who need to be forgiven for their sin. That's why God sent His very own Son in a very unordinary, miraculous way—Jesus Christ as a baby born in a manger in Bethlehem. He sent Him because every person needs a Saviour to save him from his sin.

3 Lesson Three

Jesus Is Born in Bethlehem

Theme: The arrival of Jesus is the greatest of miracles.

 ## Scripture

Memory Verse

Luke 2:11
"For unto you is born this day in the city of David a Saviour, which is Christ the Lord."

Luke 2:1–18

1   And it came to pass in those days, that there went out a decree from Caesar Augustus, that all the world should be taxed.

2   (And this taxing was first made when Cyrenius was governor of Syria.)

3   And all went to be taxed, every one into his own city.

4   And Joseph also went up from Galilee, out of the city of Nazareth, into Judaea, unto the city of David, which is called Bethlehem; (because he was of the house and lineage of David:)

5   To be taxed with Mary his espoused wife, being great with child.

6   And so it was, that, while they were there, the days were accomplished that she should be delivered.

7   And she brought forth her firstborn son, and wrapped him in swaddling clothes, and laid him in a manger; because there was no room for them in the inn.

8   And there were in the same country shepherds abiding in the field, keeping watch over their flock by night.

9   And, lo, the angel of the Lord came upon them, and the glory of the Lord shone round about them: and they were sore afraid.

10 And the angel said unto them, Fear not: for, behold, I bring you good tidings of great joy, which shall be to all people.

11 For unto you is born this day in the city of David a Saviour, which is Christ the Lord.

12 And this shall be a sign unto you; Ye shall find the babe wrapped in swaddling clothes, lying in a manger.

13 And suddenly there was with the angel a multitude of the heavenly host praising God, and saying,

14 Glory to God in the highest, and on earth peace, good will toward men.

15 And it came to pass, as the angels were gone away from them into heaven, the shepherds said one to another, Let us now go even unto Bethlehem,

and see this thing which is come to pass, which the Lord hath made known unto us.

16 *And they came with haste, and found Mary, and Joseph, and the babe lying in a manger.*

17 *And when they had seen it, they made known abroad the saying which was told them concerning this child.*

18 *And all they that heard it wondered at those things which were told them by the shepherds.*

Teacher's Checklist

- ❑ Read Luke 2:1–18 daily.
- ❑ Study Lesson Three.
- ❑ Flash cards 3.1–3.3
- ❑ Prepare snack—Cake Mix Cookies.
- ❑ Gather for object lesson—shoe box with a lid, Christmas wrapping, ribbon, Nativity scene, sheep, scroll, cross, candy.
- ❑ Gather for game—new or recycled Christmas cards.
- ❑ Print and duplicate Coloring Pages or Activity Pages on the Ministry Resource CD (one per student).
- ❑ Purchase for craft—popsicle sticks, craft wood shapes, fabric.
- ❑ Gather for craft—magnets, crayons.
- ❑ Print and duplicate the Take-Home Paper on the Ministry Resource CD (one per student).

Snack Suggestion

Cake mix cookies wrapped with shoe string licorice
Use a funfetti cake mix or your favorite cake mix. Recipe: 1 cake mix, 1/3 cup vegetable oil, and 2 eggs. Combine ingredients. Roll mix onto wax paper. Use a square cookie cutter to cut into "gift box" shape. Put square shapes on an ungreased pan. Bake @ 375 degrees for 10 minutes or until golden brown. Place the licorice on the square cookie as a bow.

 **Bible Lesson**

Scripture: Luke 2:1–18

INTRODUCING THE STORY

If you were going to choose a miracle for God to do in your life or the life of someone you love, what miracle would you choose? (Teacher, allow time for students to answer.)

If you were blind, what miracle would you hope for? (Most children will answer "sight.") Jesus performed miracles and gave sight to four blind men in the Bible. Imagine, being blind—not being able to see anything—and then Jesus comes and heals your eyes so you can see everything! You would think that was the greatest miracle God could ever do.

If you were hungry, and you had no food, no money, and no one there to give you something to eat, and you felt like you were starving, what miracle would you hope for? (Children will answer "food.") Jesus performed a miracle and fed over five thousand people with just a few loaves of bread and a two fish. Another time, He fed over four thousand people in the same way. He multiplied the bread and the fish to feed thousands of people! Imagine being hungry, with no hope of food in sight, and then Jesus comes and feeds you and everyone else with food He made out of practically nothing! You would think that was the greatest miracle God could ever do.

Jesus performed other miracles when He lived on earth. He turned water into wine. He healed lame people, deaf people, and other people who had all sorts of diseases. He gave fishermen a huge catch of fish in their nets when they had caught no fish all night, He walked on top of the water in the middle of a storm, and He put money inside a fish for the disciples to catch and pay their taxes. Jesus did many miracles, and the people for whom He did them likely thought that the miracle He did in their lives was the greatest miracle God could ever do.

There is one miracle that everyone who has ever lived needed God to do, and we are going to learn about that miracle today. That miracle was not just for a blind man, a lame man, or a deaf man. It was not just for a fisherman, a disciple who had no money to pay his taxes, or for a hungry man. That miracle was for all people, of all time, in every place in the world. We are going to learn about the greatest miracle of all time.

 Teacher's Note

Miracle: a deviation from the known laws of nature; a supernatural event

 Teaching Tip

The accounts of these miracles of restored sight are found in Matthew 9:27–30, Mark 8:22–25, & John 9:1–7. The accounts of the loaves and fishes are found in Matthew 14:15–21 & Matthew 15:32–38.

THE STORY

Flash Card 3.1

Teaching Tip

Show students a map of Palestine during the life of Christ, so they can see the distance between Nazareth and Bethlehem.

1. The Trip to Bethlehem (vv. 1–5)

Joseph and Mary, whom we learned about last week, started out on a long journey to the city of Bethlehem. Everyone was required by the Roman government to go to the city where his or her family was originally from in order to give their names to the proper officers and to be taxed. Joseph's and Mary's families were from Bethlehem, so that is the city to which they journeyed.

"I just wish our first trip to Bethlehem together didn't have to be such a hard journey for Mary," Joseph thought as he got their belongings together for the eighty-mile trip. "I can't imagine how difficult this trip will be for Mary, being so close to delivering the baby. I'll take the best care of her as I know how."

"Mary, let's get started. We want to get to Bethlehem before the crowds arrive, so we can get a room in an inn," Joseph spoke gently to his wife.

Soon Joseph and Mary were on their way to Bethlehem. The trip was long, and slower than usual, as Mary couldn't travel quickly, being so close to delivering the baby.

Many people were traveling to Bethlehem, and Joseph and Mary enjoyed talking with old friends who passed them on the way.

Four days later, Joseph and Mary arrived in Bethlehem, tired and ready to rest. They stopped at an inn to rent a room. No room. They stopped at another, and another; and still, no room. Most of the travelers had been able to make the trip more quickly than Joseph and Mary, and they had rented all the rooms in Bethlehem before Joseph and Mary arrived.

Joseph was a good man, and he loved Mary dearly. He asked every person he could find, "Do you have a room we could rent—my wife is great with child, and the baby will arrive soon." Still, no rooms.

Finally, one of the innkeepers said, "I don't have a room, but I will share what I have with you. I see your wife needs to have a safe place to rest. I have a stable, where the travelers keep their donkeys—it's not much, but at least it has a roof and warm straw. You're welcome to stay there."

Joseph thanked the innkeeper, and he settled his wife into the stable for the night.

2. The Birth of Jesus (vv. 6–7)

There they were, sleeping in a stable—a barn for animals! Joseph and Mary were poor, but they had never slept in a stable before, and Mary was expecting a baby any day now. Although their circumstances were not what they would have chosen for themselves, they knew God would take care of them, just as He always had.

"And so it was, that, while they were there, the days were accomplished that she should be delivered" (v. 6). The time had come for Mary's baby to be delivered, and they were still in the stable—still no room in the inns. But Joseph and Mary knew God was taking care of them, and they trusted His plan for them, just as they always had. They knew God had a special plan for this baby.

"And she brought forth her firstborn son, and wrapped him in swaddling clothes, and laid him in a manger; because there was no room for them in the inn" (v. 7). There, in the barn, Mary gave birth to Jesus, the Saviour of the world! She wrapped Him in swaddling clothes, and she laid Him in the manger where the cows and horses ate their hay. And Joseph named Him Jesus, just as the angel had told him to do all those months earlier, when he spoke to Joseph in a dream.

There was no bassinet, no cradle, no crib for the baby Jesus. There were no doctors or nurses to care for Him and His mother. There were no soft sheets, no blankets, no cozy sleepers for Him. There were no friends to come visit and say, "Isn't He cute? He looks just like His mother!"

But, there He was in a manger in Bethlehem, the place God had long ago told the prophets He was to be born.

Micah 5:2

2   *But thou, Bethlehem Ephratah, though thou be little among the thousands of Judah, yet out of thee shall he come forth unto me that is to be ruler in Israel; whose goings forth have been from of old, from everlasting.*

Matthew 2:5–6

5   *And they said unto him, In Bethlehem of Judaea: for thus it is written by the prophet,*

6   *And thou Bethlehem, in the land of Juda, art not the least among the princes of Juda: for out of thee shall come a Governor, that shall rule my people Israel.*

Flash Card 3.2

Teacher's Note

Swaddle: to bind tight with clothes; used generally of infants; as, to swaddle a child. **Swaddling-clothes:** a band or cloth wrapped around an infant (like a receiving blanket).

Act It Out

Bring a doll and a receiving blanket to class, and wrap the doll in the receiving blanket as you explain swaddling clothes.

Teacher's Note

Prophet: a person illuminated, inspired or instructed by God to announce future events

He was there with His mother, Mary, her husband, Joseph; and, best of all, God, His Father watching over them all.

Jesus' birth was a miracle! God had told the prophets many years earlier that the Messiah (the Saviour) would be born without an earthly father. This had never happened before, and it would never happen again; but it happened that night in a stable in Bethlehem. Jesus' mother, a virgin, gave birth to the Saviour of the world—the Son of God!

Flash Card 3.3

3. The Shepherds Receive a Birth Announcement (vv. 8–14)

That very night, on a hillside near Bethlehem, a bright light shone through the darkness of the night sky. An angel's voice rang out, clear in the night, calling to a group of shepherds and awakening their sheep. The shepherds were filled with fright.

"And the angel said unto them, Fear not: for, behold, I bring you good tidings of great joy, which shall be to all people. For unto you is born this day in the city of David a Saviour, which is Christ the Lord" (vv. 10–11). The angel was saying to the shepherds, "Don't be afraid at all! I have wonderful news that will fill your hearts with joy. The Messiah—the one who has come to take away your sin—has been born. He is nearby, in Bethlehem, the city of David.

"You will be sure to recognize Him, because He is the only newborn baby in Bethlehem who was born in a stable. He is lying there, right now, wrapped in swaddling clothes—in a manger! God wanted you to be some of the very first people to receive the joyful news."

Soon the whole bright midnight sky was filled with angels! They had come to tell the shepherds and the whole world about the miracle of Jesus' birth. "And suddenly there was with the angel a multitude of the heavenly host praising God, and saying, Glory to God in the highest, and on earth peace, good will toward men" (vv. 13–14). The birth of Jesus was such a special miracle that God sent His very own messengers from Heaven to tell the good news.

4. The Shepherds Go to See the Baby (vv. 15–16)

After the angels went back into Heaven, the shepherds talked excitedly among themselves. "Let's go into the city of Bethlehem right away and see this baby.

Can you imagine—God told us about the miracle of the Christ child's birth—us, just poor shepherds?"

"And they came with haste, and found Mary, and Joseph, and the babe lying in a manger" (v. 16). The shepherds hurried into Bethlehem, and they found the stable where Mary, Joseph, and baby Jesus were. It was just an ordinary stable. Inside the ordinary stable were ordinary animals—camels, donkeys, and a few sheep. There was ordinary straw on the floor. Everything about the stable was very ordinary.

But in this ordinary stable, in the ordinary manger from which the ordinary animals usually ate, lay a very extraordinary baby—the greatest miracle of all time! The Saviour of the world, the Son of God, born of a virgin, was in that stable.

The shepherds stood by the manger and looked at the newborn baby. A hush came over all of them. "This is the very Son of God. This is the greatest miracle of all time. This is our Saviour. And God told us about Him." The shepherds thanked God for sending Jesus and for sending the angels to them.

5. The Shepherds Share the Good News (vv. 17–18)

The shepherds couldn't keep this miracle to themselves, and God didn't want them to keep it to themselves. As they headed back to their fields, they told everyone they met about the miracle they had just been shown. They told them the Messiah, the Saviour of the world, had just been born, and they had seen Him with their own eyes. They told about the angel and the group of angels who praised God and told them about the baby. They told everyone they saw everything they had heard and seen.

6. Mary Thinks About What Happened (v. 19)

Back in the stable, Mary thought about what had happened. She thought about the angel who had first told her that she was going to give birth to the Son of God. She thought about the angel who had come to Joseph and told him that he should not be afraid to take Mary for his wife—that the child to whom she would give birth was the Son of God. She thought about the prophecies she had read in the Bible about Jesus—that He would be born of

Teacher's Note

Prophecy: a foretelling; a prediction; a declaration of something to come. As only God knows future events with certainty, no being but God or some person informed by Him can utter a real prophecy.

a virgin in Bethlehem. She thought about how God had brought her and Joseph to Bethlehem at just the right time for the baby to be born. It was just as God had said. She thought about the angels and the shepherds. She thought about the stable, the manger, and the baby.

"It's the greatest miracle there ever has been or ever will be," Mary thought. "And to think, God used me—a poor, ordinary Jewish woman—to bring His Son, the greatest miracle of all time, into the world."

7. The Shepherds Praise God (v. 20)

When the shepherds arrived back on the hillside, they talked about what had just happened.

"The night had been so dark and quiet," said one, "and then, all of a sudden, it was filled with light."

"And the angel," said another, "knew we would be afraid. I mean, who wouldn't be afraid? Here we are, a bunch of ordinary shepherds on an ordinary night, taking care of our ordinary sheep on an ordinary hillside. And then, out of nowhere comes this unordinary angel, and along with it an amazing, extraordinary light from Heaven. Who wouldn't be scared?"

"So the angel says, 'Don't be afraid. The Saviour is born in Bethlehem, and you are going to be able to recognize Him!'"

"Can you believe it?" asked another shepherd. " Can you believe that God wanted to tell us first—ordinary shepherds—about the miraculous birth of the Saviour?"

And all the shepherds thanked God for what He had showed them and told them and that He had sent His Son—the Saviour of the world.

APPLYING THE STORY

Of all the miracles God ever performed, the birth of Jesus in Bethlehem was the greatest. The miracle of Jesus' birth was for all people, in all places, for all time. And, just as this greatest miracle was for ordinary people (the ordinary shepherds taking care of ordinary sheep on the ordinary hillside), this greatest miracle is for you and me—ordinary people.

It is for ordinary dads, moms, boys, and girls. It is for ordinary teachers, electricians, doctors, and pastors. It is for ordinary lawyers, plumbers, painters, and secretaries. It is for ordinary children sitting in this Sunday school class on this ordinary Sunday. It is for you!

The thing about ordinary people (which is all people in the world) is that they are sinners who need to be forgiven for their sin. That's why God sent His very own Son in a very unordinary, miraculous way—Jesus Christ as a baby born in a manger in Bethlehem. He sent Him because every person needs a Saviour to save him from his sin.

When God created the first man and the first woman, Adam and Eve, about six thousand years ago, He planned for them to honor Him and obey Him. He planned to have a close relationship with them, in which they knew Him and knew how much He loved them. He knew what was best for them, and He knew what would make their lives happy.

God told Adam and Eve that if they disobeyed Him—if they sinned— they would have to die. That death didn't only mean that their bodies would die and be buried in the ground; it also meant that their spirits—the part of them that knew God personally—would die. It also meant that they would have to suffer eternal punishment in a real place, a lake of fire that the Bible calls Hell.

Well, Adam and Eve did disobey God. They sinned, and that meant that their spirits died, and their bodies would have to die some day. That meant they would have to suffer eternal punishment.

Since that time, every person has inherited Adam's sin nature, and every person has sinned. Every person disobeys or lies or cheats or steals. Everyone sins. Because of our sin, we have to die, too. One day our bodies will die, and one day we will have to suffer eternal punishment for our sin.

But God loved Adam and Eve, and God loves us. He didn't want us to have to suffer eternal punishment. He wanted us to be with Him forever, just like He had planned when He created Adam and Eve. Right after Adam and Eve sinned, God promised He would one day send a Saviour to pay for the sin of every person who trusts in Him.

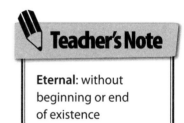

Teacher's Note

Eternal: without beginning or end of existence

Teacher's Note

Inherit: to take by descent from an ancestor

Genesis 3:15

15 *And I will put enmity between thee and the woman, and between thy seed and her seed; it shall bruise thy head, and thou shalt bruise his heel.*

John 3:16

16 *For God so loved the world, that he gave his only begotten*

Son, that whosoever believeth in him should not perish, but have everlasting life.

Those who would trust in this Saviour would be forgiven for their sin, and they would not suffer eternal punishment for their sin. They would go to Heaven when they die.

About four thousand years passed after Adam and Eve disobeyed God, and everyone who believed that God would keep His promise to send a Saviour was forgiven for their sin and went to Heaven when they died. Everyone who didn't believe God would send the Saviour—who didn't trust in Him—had to suffer eternal punishment in Hell when they died.

Then, just as we learned today, on one miraculous night that changed the world forever, God sent the promised Saviour—His own Son. That baby, lying in a manger in a stable in Bethlehem, would one day die to pay for the sins of every man, woman, boy and girl in the whole world. All they would have to do to have their sins forgiven was to trust in the Saviour who was born and died to pay the price for their sins.

This miracle was for you. You have sinned. You will have to die one day. Will you trust in the Saviour—the miraculously born Son of God—as the payment for your sin? When you trust Jesus as your Saviour, He changes your ordinary life into a very unordinary life of knowing Him. If you would like to trust Jesus as your Saviour, or if you don't really understand what I am talking about and want to ask me questions about it, you can talk to me after class is over.

If your life is already unordinary—because you have trusted in the Saviour, the Lord Jesus Christ, as the payment for your sin—there is another message for you in this miraculous story. What did the shepherds do after they saw and heard the angels and after they saw baby Jesus, the Son of God, in the manger? (Teacher, allow students to answer.) The shepherds were so thankful that the Messiah had finally come, that they told everyone they met what they had seen and heard. They told everyone about Jesus.

And that is what God wants us to do. He wants each of us to tell other people about Jesus and that He has forgiven our sin. He wants us to tell them that He loves them and wants to forgive their sin as well. He wants us to share the Good News with them, just as the shepherds did on that miraculous night that changed them and that changed the world. Then, God will use you as the messenger to bring the news that will change someone else's life forever.

Review Game/Questions

Christmas Card Review Game

Materials needed

New or recycled Christmas cards

Set up

Before class, print out and cut each question and the point values. Glue or tape them to the inside of a Christmas card. Points go on top or on the left side of the Christmas card and the question is taped or glued to the bottom or right side of the Christmas card. Display Christmas cards in front of the class (on wall, chalkboard tray, or standing on a table).

Playing the Game

Divide class into teams. Call on a student to come to the front of class and pick a Christmas card. The student opens the card and says… "For _____ (the amount of points printed on the inside) points," and then reads the question. The student then can call on a team member to answer the question. If the answer is correct, they receive those points. The team with the most points wins the game.

Variations

1. Play individually. Instead of putting points on the inside of the card, place a number 1–10. The student who picks the card and answers correctly, gets that many pieces of small candy.
2. The student who picks the card must also answer the question.

1. Why did Joseph and Mary travel to Bethlehem?
    Answer: To be taxed

2. When Joseph and Mary arrived in Bethlehem, could they find a room that was available for the night?
    Answer: No

3. Where was Jesus born in Bethlehem?
    Answer: In a stable

4. What did Mary use as a cradle for Jesus?
    Answer: A manger

5. What group of people received a special visit from an angel?
    Answer: The shepherds on a hillside near Bethlehem

6. What did the angel tell the shepherds?
   Answer: The Saviour had been born in Bethlehem!

7. After the shepherds saw baby Jesus in the manger, what did they do?
   Answer: They told everyone that Jesus Christ was born.

8. After Jesus was born and the shepherds left the stable, what did Mary do?
   Answer: She thought about and pondered everything that happened.

9. What is the greatest miracle ever performed?
   Answer: The birth of Jesus in Bethlehem

10. Once we have experienced the miracle of salvation, what should we do?
    Answer: Tell others about Jesus and His forgiveness of sins.

The Steps of Our Saviour | © 2011 Striving Together Publications

Teaching the Memory Verse

Luke 2:11

11 For unto you is born this day in the city of David a Saviour, which is Christ the Lord.

Motions

- **Luke 2:11**
- **For**—Hold up four fingers
- **unto you**—Point to the class
- **is born**—Cradle a baby
- **this day**—Begin with arms folded left hand over right elbow. Then lift left hand as if the sun were rising
- **in the city**—With your finger outline the city skyline
- **of David**—Place crown on head
- **a Saviour,**—Make cross with two fingers
- **which is Christ the Lord.**—Show class pointer finger. Then point to heaven.

Teaching the Memory Verse:

The prophecy was fulfilled. Just like God promised, He sent us a Saviour. The place was right, and the time was right.

Object Lesson—Christmas Box

Props: Select a box and decorate it with Christmas wrappings and ribbons. For the lesson to be most effective, it should be very easy to get the lid off the box. You might use a shoe box, wrapping the lid separately from the box so you can quickly untie a ribbon and lift off the lid.

The following objects should be inside the box: a Nativity scene manger, a small doll representing Baby Jesus, a sheep, a scroll, a cross, and a small unwrapped gift (perhaps a piece of candy or an inexpensive ornament) for each child.

Lesson: What's your favorite time of year? Lots of us like Christmas better than any other time of year. One of our favorite things about Christmas is the gifts! Brightly colored packages with ribbons and lots of tape are great fun to open.

(Hold gift box up and turn it around to display all sides.) I think my gift is very pretty, don't you? Some gifts are almost too pretty to open! This one would make a pretty decoration. But my curiosity always gets the best of me. I simply must find out what's inside.

(Begin to untie the ribbon.) I hope this is something really special! What is the best gift you've ever received? I've gotten many nice gifts. It would be hard to pick a favorite.

(Lift the lid off the box.) This is interesting.

(Lift out the manger.) This is a manger—a place where farmers put the feed for cows to eat.

(Pass the manger around for each child to hold—wait for the manger to get back to you before you continue.) Look at this!

(Lift out the small doll.) Since the beginning of the world, people have wondered what God is like. On the first Christmas, Jesus came to Earth. He was born in a stable. His mother wrapped Him up and laid Him in a manger.

(Pass the doll around for each child to hold—wait for it to come back before you continue.) God put a special star in the sky that night and He sent angels to show the way to the manger.

(Lift out the sheep.) There were some shepherds spending the night out in fields taking care of their sheep that night.

(Pass the sheep around for each child to hold.) Most people thought shepherds were not very important people. God sent an angel to come and tell them that Jesus was born. The shepherds were afraid when they saw a real angel. But the angel told them not to be afraid because he had good news for them. The angel invited the shepherds to see Baby Jesus in the manger. And God sent a whole sky full of angels to celebrate Jesus' birth. When I look at this sheep, I remember that God loves us all—even when other people don't think we are very important, we are important to God.

(Lift the scroll out of the box.) Back then, the Bible was written on scrolls like this one. (Of course the only part of the Bible they had was the Old Testament. The New Testament was written later to tell us about Jesus.) A very long time before Jesus was born, God told the Old Testament prophets to tell every one that Jesus was coming. They wrote down what God said—that Jesus was coming to save us from our sin.

(Pass the scroll around for the children to see, wait for it to come back before you continue.) God wants us to always love each other and be kind to each other. But we often want to do things our own way even if we hurt someone else by what we are doing. When we do things our own way instead of God's way, we sin. For example, when we say or do something unkind to another child, that is sin. When we disobey our parents, that is sin. When we say something that is not true, that is sin. The Bible says that we all sin. Sin is like a wall that keeps us away from God. When we sin, someone has to be punished for it. God knew that we could not stand to be punished for all of our own sins. God loves us so much that He sent Jesus to take away our sin.

(Lift the cross out of the box.) When Jesus died on the cross, He took the punishment for all of our sins. On the cross, Jesus paid for all my sin. On the cross, Jesus paid for all of your sins.

(Pass the cross around and wait for it to come back to you.) Jesus died on the cross, but He did not stay dead. God raised Jesus back to life. Right now, Jesus is alive. He lives in Heaven and, if we ask Him to, He will also live in our hearts. When I asked Jesus to come into my heart, I accepted the gift from God. The Bible says that when I accepted this gift I became a child of God because I believed on Jesus. All my sins got washed away, and I get to spend forever with God in Heaven. This is a gift that God offers to each of us. There is a small gift in this box for each of you.

(Remove one gift from the box and give it to the first child saying, "Sue, this is a gift for you, will you accept it?" When the child agrees, give the gift. Repeat for each child.) Each of you accepted the gift. What if someone said, "No, I don't want the gift"? You can only take a gift with you if you accept it. It's the same with Jesus' gift to you. It only belongs to you if you accept it.

Craft—Jesus Is Born Magnet

Getting It Together

Popsicle sticks
Craft wood shapes
Fabric
Glue
Magnets
Crayons

Putting It Together

1. Give each child 10 popsicle sticks, crayons, pieces of fabric, and 3 wooden circles.
2. Have each student color the popsicle sticks brown.
3. Glue 3 sticks together making a triangle (roof).
4. Glue 6 sticks side-by-side onto the bottom of the triangle (making the stable).
5. Glue 1 stick onto the bottom of the stable.
6. Have the students glue fabric onto the wooden circles making Joseph, Mary, and baby Jesus.
7. Glue them onto the stable.
8. Glue the magnet on the back.

Seeing It Together

The greatest miracle occurred when God became flesh and dwelt among us. Jesus, the Creator, humbled Himself and arrived in the form of a baby so that we could have eternal life. As the students color and glue the craft together, ask how the birth of Jesus has changed their lives.

Additional Resources

Find the following items on the Ministry Resource CD:

- Coloring Page (for younger children)
- Activity Page (for older children)
- Student Take-Home Paper
- PowerPoint Presentation

Suggested Classroom Schedule

Before Class	Complete attendance record. Provide students with coloring pages/activity pages.
Opening	Welcome
Prayer	Prayer requests and praise reports from the children
Song Time	
Memory Verse	Psalm 96:8
Song Time	
Object Lesson	Wise Men Still Seek Him
Bible Lesson	The Wise Men Visit Jesus
Application/Invitation	Help saved students apply lesson. Invite unsaved students to receive Christ.
Snack	Star-shaped Cookies
Review Game/ Questions	Stars and Points
Craft	Wise Men Nativity Set
Closing	Give announcements and pray. Distribute take home-papers.

Lesson Four Overview

The Wise Men Visit Jesus
Theme—Jesus is worthy of our best gifts.

Scripture
Matthew 2:1–12

Memory Verse
Psalm 96:8—*"Give unto the LORD the glory due unto his name: bring an offering, and come into his courts."*

Lesson Outline

Introducing the Story
What is the best gift you gave to someone else for Christmas? In our story today, we will learn from some gift-givers in the Bible what makes a gift really special.

Telling the Story
1. Jesus Is Born in Bethlehem *(v.1)*

2. **Wise Men Follow the Star to Search for Jesus** *(vv.1–2)*
   —Flash Card 4.1

3. **King Herod Gathers Together Priests and Scribes**
   (vv. 3–6, Micah 5:2)—Flash Card 4.2

4. **Herod Sends for Wise Men** *(vv. 7–8, Matthew 2:13b)*

5. **Wise Men Continue to Follow the Star to Jesus**
   (vv. 9–10, Psalm 105:3)

6. **Wise Men Worship Jesus and Give Him Gifts** *(v.11)*
   —Flash Card 4.3

7. **Wise Men Return Home Another Way** *(v.12)*

Applying the Story
When you give your heart to Jesus, you, like the wise men, will have given Him your very best. What are some things you can do to help people get to Jesus?

4 Lesson Four

The Wise Men Visit Jesus

Theme: Jesus is worthy of our best gifts.

Scripture

Matthew 2:1–12

1   Now when Jesus was born in Bethlehem of Judaea in the days of Herod the king, behold, there came wise men from the east to Jerusalem,

2   Saying, Where is he that is born King of the Jews? for we have seen his star in the east, and are come to worship him.

3   When Herod the king had heard these things, he was troubled, and all Jerusalem with him.

4   And when he had gathered all the chief priests and scribes of the people together, he demanded of them where Christ should be born.

5   And they said unto him, In Bethlehem of Judaea: for thus it is written by the prophet,

6   And thou Bethlehem, in the land of Juda, art not the least among the princes of Juda: for out of thee shall come a Governor, that shall rule my people Israel.

7   Then Herod, when he had privily called the wise men, enquired of them diligently what time the star appeared.

8   And he sent them to Bethlehem, and said, Go and search diligently for the young child; and when ye have found him, bring me word again, that I may come and worship him also.

9   When they had heard the king, they departed; and, lo, the star, which they saw in the east, went before them, till it came and stood over where the young child was.

10   When they saw the star, they rejoiced with exceeding great joy.

11   And when they were come into the house, they saw the young child with Mary his mother, and fell down, and worshipped him: and when they had opened their treasures, they presented unto him gifts; gold, and frankincense and myrrh.

12   And being warned of God in a dream that they should not return to Herod, they departed into their own country another way.

Memory Verse

Psalm 96:8
"Give unto the LORD the glory due unto his name: bring an offering, and come into his courts."

Teacher's Checklist

Snack Suggestion

Star-shaped Cookies
Bake star-shaped sugar cookies and decorate with sprinkles or bright décor. Consider allowing children to decorate their cookie stars in class.

❑ Read Matthew 2:1–12 daily.

❑ Study Lesson Four.

❑ Flash cards 4.1–4.3

❑ Prepare snack—Star-shaped Cookies.

❑ Print "Stars" from the Ministry Resource CD.

❑ Gather for object lesson—Smarties candy.

❑ Gather for craft—crayons and scissors.

❑ Print and duplicate Coloring Pages or Activity Pages on the Ministry Resource CD (one per student).

❑ Print and duplicate Take-Home Paper on the Ministry Resource CD (one per student).

Bible Lesson

Scripture: Matthew 2:1–12

INTRODUCING THE STORY

Often, right after Christmas, someone will ask you, "What is the best gift you received for Christmas?" Then, you might think for a moment, or, you might not have to think before you answer, because you received the exact gift you had been wanting. Whether you had to think about it, or you had it right in the front of your mind because you got exactly what you wanted, you answer the person. You might smile and say, "I got a bike" or "I got an outfit" or "I got a game" or "I got a doll," or whatever your favorite gift was. (Allow students time to talk about their favorite gifts.)

What if I were to ask you, "What is the best gift you gave to someone else for Christmas?" or "What is your favorite gift you have ever given to someone?" How would you answer? Is there a gift for which you had to save your money for a long time in order to buy it? Is there a gift you have worked for and thought about so much that you just couldn't wait until it was time for the person to open it? Is there a gift you have given that gave you more happiness to give than you have ever felt receiving a gift? Who did you give it to, and what was that gift? (Again, allow students to answer.)

In our story today, we will learn from some gift-givers in the Bible what makes a gift really special.

THE STORY

1. Jesus Is Born in Bethlehem (v. 1)

The past few weeks we have learned about the birth of Jesus, and we have learned that His birth was the greatest miracle of all time.

We talked about Jesus' cousin, John the Baptist—we learned that he was born to parents who were really too old to have a baby. But God performed a miracle, and John was born to Zacharias and Elisabeth. We learned that John was the last prophet to tell people that the Messiah—the Saviour they had been waiting for—was coming to save them from their sins.

We learned about the angel coming first to Mary, and then Joseph, telling them that Mary was going to have a baby, and that her baby would be the Son of God. Mary's baby would be the Saviour whom God had promised to the world. We learned that the angel told Joseph to name the baby Jesus.

We studied about Jesus' birth in a stable in the city of Bethlehem. We learned that God had prophesied many years earlier that Jesus would be born in Bethlehem, and that He would be born of a virgin. We learned that the birth of Jesus happened just as God had said it would.

We talked about the angels coming to shepherds on a hillside near Bethlehem and telling them that the Saviour was finally born. We learned that the shepherds not only went to see Baby Jesus, but afterward they went and told everyone about the wonderful things they had seen and heard.

Today we will learn what some other people did when they heard that Jesus was born.

Flash Card 4.1

🔦 Teaching Tip

If you have a portable telescope, bring it to class. Look through the telescope as you talk about the wise men studying the stars, and in particular, the star that led to the Saviour.

Alternately (and more simple), cover a paper towel roll in foil and hold it up to your eye, as if looking at the star through a scope at appropriate points throughout the story.

2. Wise Men Follow the Star to Search for Jesus (vv. 1–2)

When Jesus was born, there was a group of men who lived in a country far to the east of Judaea, the land where Jesus was born. These were very wise and important men in their country. They gave counsel to the rulers of the countries of the east.

These men, called wise men, were highly educated. They studied math. They studied science. They studied the stars. They studied all the religions of the world. As they studied different religions, they realized they were not happy. There was something missing in their lives. The gods they worshipped were false gods, and their gods didn't give them peace in their hearts. Their gods didn't love them or give them hope. Their gods were idols, made out of wood and stone. Their gods left them feeling empty.

As the wise men studied religions, they studied the Bible in order to learn about the God of the Bible. In the Bible, they found many prophecies that told about a king who was going to be born—the King of the Jews. The Bible said that this King would also be a Saviour to save people from their sins. "We must learn more about this King and Saviour," thought the wise men.

One night, the wise men noticed something they had never seen before as they looked up at the sky. The wise men knew all the stars that were usually in the night sky over their land—they had studied them all. But tonight, as these wise men from the east gazed at the western sky, over the land of Judaea there was a star that had never been there before—a star different than any other. The star shone so brightly and had a glow unlike any of the other stars, and it caused the wise men to think.

"What is the significance of this amazing star?" the wise men wondered. Then, they remembered what they had read in the Bible, and they ran to the scrolls to look at it again. Yes, there it was. The King about whom they had read—the King of the Jews—would be born in the land of Judaea.

Suddenly, nothing was as important to the wise men as finding the King of the Jews and worshipping Him. They stopped everything they were doing, and they prepared to follow the star to the one about whom they had read in the Bible.

"We'll follow it," they said to each other. "We will follow that amazing star all the way until we find the King of the Jews, and we will worship Him."

The men packed up clean clothes and food for their journey. They brushed their camels and filled the camels' packs with all the supplies they would need along the way.

Deep in their hearts, the wise men believed that the God they had studied about in the Bible was the true God. "What can we give Him to bring honor to Him?" they wondered. "What can we give to the newborn King, the Messiah, the Saviour?"

"We'll give the best our land has to offer. We will give gifts fit for the King that He is." So, they packed the most precious things they possessed to give the baby King—gold, frankincense, and myrrh.

The wise men walked mile after mile, keeping their eyes on the star as they journeyed. They knew the star was going to lead them to the Saviour about whom they had read, and they would let nothing keep them from finding Him and worshipping Him. They looked forward to arriving in Judaea and taking part in all the celebrations that would be honoring the newborn King.

Finally, the wise men arrived in Judaea. But there were no celebrations—no trumpets, no singers, no feasts. In fact, it looked to the wise men like the people of Judaea, the Israelites, didn't even know that their King had been born.

"Where is your newborn King?" they asked a farmer in his field. The farmer didn't know—he hadn't even heard there was a new king.

The wise men found a woman drawing water out of a well. "Where is your newborn King?" they asked the woman. The woman said she hadn't heard anything about a new king.

The wise men went from person to person, house to house, asking where the newborn King was. "Where is he that is born King of the Jews? for we have

Teaching Tip

Make a star you can follow as you teach the lesson. You can use a decorative Christmas star or cover a homemade posterboard star with glitter or foil. Tie a string to the star and hang it from a stick or pole, much like a fishing pole. Simply hold the pole in front of you, with the star hanging from it, and let it lead you as you teach the lesson.

Alternately, you can use an overhead projector to illuminate a star on the wall, and walk toward it at appropriate points throughout the lesson.

seen his star in the east, and are come to worship him" (v. 2). But no one knew where He was.

Flash Card 4.2

3. King Herod Gathers Together Priests and Scribes (vv. 3–6)

When Herod, the cruel and wicked king of Judaea, heard of the wise men coming to Judaea and asking where the newborn King of the Jews was, King Herod was afraid. "Will He try to take over my throne?" thought King Herod. "Will the people follow Him instead of me?"

King Herod called the religious rulers of his kingdom—the ones who had studied the Bible. "Tell me where it is prophesied that Christ will be born," he demanded.

"And they said unto him, In Bethlehem of Judaea: for thus it is written by the prophet…" (v. 5). "The King of the Jews, the Christ, will be born in Bethlehem, according to what the prophet wrote in the Bible," the wise men told King Herod.

Micah 5:2

2   But thou, Bethlehem Ephratah, though thou be little among the thousands of Judah, yet out of thee shall he come forth unto me that is to be ruler in Israel; whose goings forth have been from of old, from everlasting.

4. Herod Sends for Wise Men (vv. 7–8)

"Find these wise men who are seeking the King of the Jews," commanded King Herod. The wise men, excited that they would finally be able to find the location of the newborn King—for certainly the king of Judaea would know where He was—gladly went to meet King Herod.

"Tell me about this star you are following," asked King Herod. "Tell me everything you know about it. When did you first see it? Where did you first see it? Did it actually bring you right here, to Judaea?"

The wise men answered the king's questions. Then, King Herod told the wise men to go to Bethlehem and search for the child. King Herod said, "When you have found Him, come and tell me exactly where He is, so I can worship Him, too."

In his heart, the wicked king Herod was thinking something totally different than he said to the wise men. "When these men find the baby, they will tell me where He is, and I will have Him killed," thought wicked King Herod. "Then He won't be able to take over my throne." But King Herod didn't tell his plan to the wise men who were looking for Jesus.

Matthew 2:13b

13b for Herod will seek the young child to destroy him.

5. Wise Men Continue to Follow the Star to Jesus (vv. 9–10)

The wise men were excited to begin the final part of their journey, and they were glad the king had told them they would find Jesus in Bethlehem. "We shall find the newborn King now," the wise men exclaimed to each other as they set out. "We know the exact city where He is."

The wise men thought other people would go with them to find the newborn King. After all, they were in His own country, and these were His own people—surely they would want to see their newborn King, now that they knew about Him!

But no one went with the wise men as they journeyed to Bethlehem. His own people weren't interested in the newborn King of the Jews. They didn't realize that their Messiah—the Son of God—had actually been born.

Then, up in the sky, appeared the same star they had followed way back when they had left their home country in the east to find the King of the Jews. The wise men were full of joy when they saw the star. This was the happiest day of their lives. "The God of Heaven has shown us His star again, leading us to the newborn King," they said to each other. "This truly must be the King of the Jews—the Messiah—for whom we are searching. The true God is leading us straight to Him by this amazing star!"

Psalm 105:3

3   Glory ye in his holy name: let the heart of them rejoice that seek the LORD.

6. Wise Men Worship Jesus and Give Him Gifts (v. 11)   Flash Card 4.3

The star led the wise men to a house in Bethlehem—Mary, Joseph, and Jesus were no longer in a stable. When they entered the house, the wise men "saw the young child with Mary his mother, and [they] fell down, and worshipped him" (v. 11).

The wise men knew immediately that this was no ordinary baby they had found. This was the King of the Jews, the Messiah, whom the true God of Heaven had promised hundreds of years earlier. This was the Saviour about whom they had read in the Bible. The men were full of amazement and wonder. This was the Son of God! The wise men fell to their knees and worshipped Jesus.

"He is worthy of the best that we have," thought the wise men. With hearts of love and adoration, they opened their bundles and laid their precious gifts—the gold, frankincense, and myrrh that they had carefully prepared for the King of the Jews—before the child. "Here you are, little King—we know you are God, the Saviour of the world—we give You our best."

7. Wise Men Return Home Another Way (v. 12)

The wise men were full of joy that they had found the King for whom they had been looking. They were now ready to return home. They wouldn't have a star to follow this time, but they knew the way home—they would just go back the same way they had come.

But, before they left, God gave the wise men a dream as they slept. "Don't return home the way you came. Don't go to King Herod. Don't let Herod know where Jesus is." So, the wise men obeyed God—the God they had now discovered was the one, true God—and they went home to their own country another way.

APPLYING THE STORY

Why did the wise men want to give precious gifts—the best gifts they had to offer—to Baby Jesus? What made them want to give to Jesus? (Students' responses will give you valuable information as to the depth of their understanding. Make sure you allow them to answer.)

The wise men wanted to give—they wanted to give their best—to Jesus because they realized who He was. They found out that He was the true God of Heaven, and they wanted to give to Him because He was their Creator, their owner, and their Saviour. They wanted to give because He loved them and they loved Him.

What did the wise men give to Jesus? (Again, wait for answers.) Yes, they gave gold, frankincense, and myrrh, but they gave other gifts to Jesus as well.

Time—The wise men gave days, weeks, and maybe months as they searched to find the King of the Jews. They gave up doing everything else they could have done with their time.

Wills—Your will is what *you* want. Your will might be to buy the latest game. Your will might be to go to a friend's house to play. Your will might be to go shopping with your mom or with friends. Whatever you want to do is your will. The wise men gave up their own wills—what they wanted—and did what God wanted. They gave up their wills and their plans when they decided to follow Jesus, and they gave up their wills when they obeyed God and returned home another way.

Hearts—The wise men gave their hearts to Jesus. When they left all they knew and all they had to seek Him, they were giving Him their hearts. When they bowed down before Jesus to worship Him, they were giving Him their hearts. When they gave Him their valuable and precious gifts, they did so because they had already given Him their hearts.

Loving God makes us want to give our best to Him. What do you have to give to Jesus? Do you have time? How would you give your best time to Jesus? You could give your best time to Jesus by spending time with Him first thing in the morning. You could give your best time to Jesus by reading your Bible and talking to Him in prayer before you eat breakfast or do other things each morning.

Do you have a will? How would you give your will to Jesus? You could give your will to Jesus by finding out what He wants you to do and then doing it. The Bible tells us what pleases God, and when we do that, rather than what we want to do, we are giving our wills to Jesus.

Do you have money? How can you give your money to Jesus? You can give money in the offering at church. You can give money to missionaries to help them share the Gospel with people in other countries. You can give money to help someone in need.

How can you give your heart to Jesus? If you are not saved, you can trust Jesus as your Saviour. If you are already saved, you can tell Him that you are all His—that you are giving every bit of yourself to Him. When you give your heart to Jesus, you are choosing to love Him and to love what He loves. When you give your heart to Jesus, you are giving Him everything.

A woman named Christina Rossetti wrote a song many years ago about giving our hearts to Jesus.

"What can I give Him,
Poor as I am?
If I were a shepherd
I would bring a lamb,
If I were a wise man,
I would do my part—
Yet what I can I give Him,
Give my heart."

When you give your heart to Jesus, you, like the wise men, will have given Him your very best.

 ## Review Game/Questions

Stars and Points
Materials Needed
Stars from the Ministry Resource CD

Set up
Print and cut out the stars from the Ministry Resource CD. Place stars in a bag. Have today's memory verse written on the chalkboard.

Playing the Game
Divide class into teams. When a student correctly answers a review question, allow him/her to pull out a star from the bag, looking for the letter on the star. That team will receive 10 points for every time that letter appears in today's memory verse. If the star does not have a letter from the memory verse, the student can choose a letter for that star (of course, encourage them to pick a letter that appears the most times). The team with the most points wins the game.

1. What group of men did we learn about in today's lesson?
    Answer: The wise men

2. As the wise men were studying the stars one night, what did they discover?
    Answer: An amazing star that would lead them to Jesus, the King of the Jews

3. Who was the cruel and wicked king of Judaea at the time?
    Answer: Herod

4. How did Herod feel about this star and the King of the Jews?
    Answer: He was scared and worried that Jesus would take over his throne.

5. What did Herod want to do to Jesus once the wise men found Him?
    Answer: Herod wanted to kill Jesus.

6. What did the wise men do when they finally saw Jesus?
    Answer: They fell down and worshipped Him.

7. What did the wise men bring for Jesus?
    Answer: Precious gifts—gold, frankincense, and myrrh

8. What message did God give the wise men in a dream?
    Answer: Don't return to King Herod. Go home a different way.

9. What other three (non-material) gifts did the wise men give to Jesus (that we can give to Him, as well!)?
    Answer: They gave of their time, wills, and hearts.

10. What other gifts can you give to Jesus?
    Answer: Answers will vary, but may include: money, talents, special possessions, etc.

Teaching the Memory Verse

Psalm 96:8

8   *Give unto the LORD the glory due unto his name: bring an offering, and come into his courts.*

Have students turn to Psalm 96:8. Read the verse as a class.

God gave us His very best—Jesus. Jesus is worthy of our best gifts. Discuss what we can give back to the Lord. Offering yourselves wholly to God declares that you worship Him only.

Write the memory verse on the chalkboard. Have the children recite the verse. Ask a child to erase a word and ask the children to repeat the verse. Continue until all the words have disappeared and the children are saying the verse from memory.

Object Lesson—Wise Men Still Seek Him

Give each child a pack of Smarties candy.

The birth of Jesus Christ caused a great interest among the rich, poor, lame and also the wise.

Matthew 2:1–2

1   *Now when Jesus was born in Bethlehem of Judaea in the days of Herod the king, behold, there came wise men from the east to Jerusalem,*

2   *Saying, Where is he that is born King of the Jews? for we have seen his star in the east, and are come to worship him.*

These Smarties will not make you smart, but I want this candy to represent the Wise Men that came to see Jesus. These men saw a bright star shining from the east and knew that God in the flesh had been born.

It doesn't matter if you are rich, poor, lame or wise, everyone must come to Jesus in order to go to Heaven. There are some people on Earth today who think they are too smart to trust Jesus as their Saviour or they think they know another way. Jesus Christ came to be born in a lowly manger so men and women, boys and girls of all types could make sure they are on their way to Heaven.

And, if you are really want to be smart, you will still seek Jesus after you are saved! You can seek Him by reading your Bible, praying, and listening to God's Word as it is taught or preached.

Craft—Wise Men Nativity Set

Getting It Together

Print out Nativity Set from the Ministry Resource CD

Putting It Together

1. Give each child a copy of the nativity set.
2. Instruct each student to cut out each character and color.

Seeing It Together

"We need to give Jesus our best gifts because He gave us the greatest gift—the gift of eternal life through Him!"

As the students assemble the craft, remind them of the gifts each character gave. What can each child give to Jesus?

Joseph—obedience
Mary—faithfulness
Shepherds—worship
Wise Men—offering
Jesus—eternal life

Additional Resources

Find the following items on the Ministry Resource CD:

- Coloring Page (for younger children)
- Activity Page (for older children)
- Student Take-Home Paper
- PowerPoint Presentation

Suggested Classroom Schedule

Before Class	Complete attendance record. Provide students with coloring pages/activity pages.
Opening	Welcome
Prayer	Prayer requests and praise reports from the children
Song Time	
Memory Verse	Luke 2:52
Song Time	
Object Lesson	Gone Missing
Bible Lesson	Jesus Visits the Temple
Application/Invitation	Help saved students apply lesson. Invite unsaved students to receive Christ.
Snack	Fruit Snacks
Review Game/Questions	Looking for Jesus
Craft	Scroll
Closing	Give announcements and pray. Distribute take-home papers.

Lesson Five Overview

Jesus Visits the Temple
Theme—Children can grow in the Lord and serve Him.

Scripture
Luke 2:41–52

Memory Verse
Luke 2:52—"And Jesus increased in wisdom and stature, and in favour with God and man."

Lesson Outline

Introducing the Story *(Romans 8:29a)*
In our story today, we are going to learn how Jesus was successful, both in the eyes of people, and in the eyes of God. Let's find out what Jesus did to be successful, so we can follow in His steps to become more like Him.

Telling the Story
1. **The Trip to Jerusalem for the Passover** *(vv. 41–42)*

2. **The Crowd Returns to Nazareth** *(v. 43, Titus 2:4–5)*

3. **Jesus Is Missing** *(vv. 44–45)—Flash Card 5.1*

4. **Jesus Is Found in the Temple** *(vv. 46–47)—Flash Card 5.2*

5. **Mary Questions Jesus** *(v. 48)*

6. **Jesus' Business** *(vv. 49–50)—Flash Card 5.3*

7. **Jesus Back Home in Nazareth** *(vv. 51–52, Hebrews 13:8, John 8:29b)*

Applying the Story *(Romans 8:6, Proverbs 9:10, 3:1–4, 1 Timothy 4:12)*
The greatest goal you can have after you are saved is to be like Jesus, and today we learned many qualities Jesus had as a child

5 Lesson Five

Jesus Visits the Temple

Theme: Children can grow in the Lord and serve Him.

 ## Scripture

Memory Verse

Luke 2:52
"And Jesus increased in wisdom and stature, and in favour with God and man."

Luke 2:41–52

41   Now his parents went to Jerusalem every year at the feast of the passover.

42   And when he was twelve years old, they went up to Jerusalem after the custom of the feast.

43   And when they had fulfilled the days, as they returned, the child Jesus tarried behind in Jerusalem; and Joseph and his mother knew not of it.

44   But they, supposing him to have been in the company, went a day's journey; and they sought him among their kinsfolk and acquaintance.

45   And when they found him not, they turned back again to Jerusalem, seeking him.

46   And it came to pass, that after three days they found him in the temple, sitting in the midst of the doctors, both hearing them, and asking them questions.

47   And all that heard him were astonished at his understanding and answers.

48   And when they saw him, they were amazed: and his mother said unto him, Son, why hast thou thus dealt with us? behold, thy father and I have sought thee sorrowing.

49   And he said unto them, How is it that ye sought me? wist ye not that I must be about my Father's business?

50   And they understood not the saying which he spake unto them.

51   And he went down with them, and came to Nazareth, and was subject unto them: but his mother kept all these sayings in her heart.

52   And Jesus increased in wisdom and stature, and in favour with God and man.

Teacher's Checklist

- ❏ Read Luke 2:41–52 daily.
- ❏ Study Lesson Five.
- ❏ Flash cards 5.1–5.3
- ❏ Prepare snack—Fruit Snacks.
- ❏ For lesson—map of Nazareth.
- ❏ Object lesson—2" x 2" cards.
- ❏ Print visuals for the review game from the Ministry Resource CD.
- ❏ Gather for memory verse review—30 balloons.
- ❏ Purchase for craft—wooden dowels.
- ❏ Gather for craft—paper.
- ❏ Print verse template for craft from the Ministry Resource CD.
- ❏ Print and duplicate Coloring Pages or Activity Pages on the Ministry Resource CD (one per student).
- ❏ Print and duplicate Take-Home Paper on the Ministry Resource CD (one per student).

Snack Suggestion

Fruit Snacks
Fruit grows as it is watered. Explain to the students how we grow spiritually through the Word of God.

Bible Lesson

Scripture: Luke 2:41–52

INTRODUCING THE STORY

If I asked you to list what makes a person successful—qualities that cause a person to be admired by other people—what would be the first quality you would choose? (Teacher, allow time for discussion. Repeat, in a thoughtful manner, each answer given by your students, and then elaborate or not, as you see fit.)

Now, what about qualities that make a person successful in God's eyes? What do you think makes a person successful to God? (You will likely receive answers such as Bible reading, prayer, soulwinning, listening to the preacher, obeying your parents, being kind, telling the truth, etc. All of these, and many more, are good answers and should be validated by your encouraging affirmation.)

In our story today, we are going to learn how Jesus was successful, both in the eyes of people, and in the eyes of God. Let's find out what Jesus did to be successful, so we can follow in His steps to become more like Him. That is God's plan for us.

Romans 8:29a

29a For whom he did foreknow, he also did predestinate to be conformed to the image of his Son.

THE STORY

1. The Trip to Jerusalem for the Passover (vv. 41–42)

Jesus was now twelve years old, and He went on a sixty-mile journey with His stepfather and mother, Joseph and Mary. They traveled by foot from their home in Nazareth to the city of Jerusalem. But they didn't make this trip alone. They went with a great crowd of people—friends and relatives—from their city. They were all going to celebrate the Passover.

The Passover is a feast that celebrates an event that had happened many years before Jesus was born. It was a special holiday during which God wanted His people to remember something wonderful He had done for them.

Teaching Tip

Compare the journey from Nazareth to Jerusalem with cities near you. "That would be like a trip from (your town) to (town 60 miles away)—walking! Can you imagine walking all the way to (town)?"

You could also show Nazareth and Jerusalem on a map.

Back in the book of Exodus (about 1,500 years earlier) God delivered His people, the Jews, from a wicked ruler in Egypt, where they were slaves. God told the Jewish people that one night all the firstborn children and animals in the land of Egypt would be killed. But God said that if the Jews would put the blood of a perfect lamb (a lamb without any cuts, wounds, or imperfections) on the doorposts of their houses, their firstborn wouldn't have to die. The death angel, who was going to kill the firstborn, would see the blood on the front of the house and would "pass over" that house; no one in any house with blood on the doorposts would have to die! That is why it is called the Passover—the death angel "passed over" the houses that had blood over the doorposts.

God wanted the Jews (and us) to remember the Passover, because He wanted us to know that it was the blood that saved them from death that night—just as it is the blood of Jesus that saves us from eternal death. The only way we can be saved from sin and death is by trusting the blood that Jesus shed for us when He died on the cross.

The journey for the Passover celebration was such a happy time for everyone, all traveling together. There were so many dads, moms, grandpas, grandmas, uncles, aunts, cousins, and friends that it was hard to count them! There was so much talking, laughing, and playing that the children wished it would never have to end.

There was also teaching on the way to Jerusalem. Many of the fathers reminded their sons about the Bible lessons they had studied throughout the year. The boys quoted to their fathers many of the Bible chapters they had memorized; Jesus quoted His chapters to Joseph. The Jewish fathers were careful to teach the Bible to their children because it was very important to them that their children knew the one true God.

Finally, this great crowd arrived in Jerusalem where they all went to the temple. Together, the Jews worshipped God there, and they ate the feast of the Passover. It was the most special time of the year between the Jews and God.

2. The Crowd Returns to Nazareth (v. 43)

Joseph and Mary loved the feast of the Passover. They loved remembering what God had done for them, and they loved thanking Him for it. They loved spending time with friends and relatives they didn't get to see very often. They were extremely happy to be part of a family that worshipped and honored God. They enjoyed talking with each other about God and the great things He had done for them.

The journey home was always something to look forward to. Hundreds of people traveled together, just as they had on the way to Jerusalem. The women had much to talk about, and they were a happy group as they set off on their way home. They knew their husbands would follow along together, as well, for the men also had much to catch up on.

The women shared recipes with each other, told cute stories about their babies, and gave each other advice about housekeeping. The older women shared with the younger women some of the lessons they had learned about being a good wife and a good mother. They talked about how to care for their gardens, what kind of perfume they wore, and the new outfits they were sewing for their children.

Titus 2:4–5

4   *That they may teach the young women to be sober, to love
     their husbands, to love their children,*

5   *To be discreet, chaste, keepers at home, good, obedient
     to their own husbands, that the word of God be
     not blasphemed.*

The men followed closely behind, talking about their jobs, their families, and the projects they were working on. They shared with each other what they were studying in the Old Testament, and they talked about what they were teaching in family devotions. They often made each other laugh with their jokes. They all had such a good time.

The children were also part of the happy group of travelers. The babies and toddlers traveled with their mothers and grandmothers, while the older children and teenagers walked along in their own group, playing games and sharing stories with each other. They loved this special trip together.

3. Jesus Is Missing (vv. 44–45)

Flash Card 5.1

As each day came to an end, and the sun began to set, the husbands would find their wives and children, and each family would settle down for the night in their own tents.

On the first evening of this particular journey home from Jerusalem, after Joseph had found Mary, he asked her, "Where's Jesus?"

"Isn't He with you?" Mary asked. "Well, I imagine He's with His cousins… I'm surprised He hasn't come looking for us, though, since it's beginning to get dark." Mary began to feel a little worried. "You know, I don't think I've seen Him since we left Jerusalem this morning."

"Well, I'm sure He's around here somewhere," Joseph answered her reassuringly. "Let's check with Zacharias and Elisabeth—He's probably with them."

Mary and Joseph went to the tent of Zacharias and Elisabeth. "Is Jesus here?" Joseph questioned Zacharias. No, they hadn't seen Jesus all day. Joseph and Mary ran over to Eli and Esther's tent. No, they hadn't seen Jesus either. Frantically now, they rushed from tent to tent, asking each person if they knew where Jesus was. Nobody had seen Jesus all day!

"How could I have let this happen?" cried Mary. "He's only twelve years old—I should have kept my eye on Him. Oh, what has happened to Him?" Mary put her face in her hands and wept.

Joseph put his strong arm around his wife. "Mary, I'm so sorry this has happened. Don't blame yourself—it's not your fault. I'm responsible, too. We both should have made sure He was with our group. He has always obeyed us and done exactly what we have said—I never even thought about the possibility of Him not just following as we began our journey back to Nazareth.

"We'll go back to Jerusalem right away. We'll follow the exact roads we have traveled so far, and we'll find Him! Don't you worry—we won't give up until we find Jesus."

And Mary and Joseph began the journey back to Jerusalem.

Joseph asked every person they met along the way to Jerusalem, "Have you seen our son, Jesus? He's a fine-looking boy, twelve years old. He was wearing a blue robe. He's always polite and helpful. Well, He's just the nicest boy you've ever met. I know you would recognize Him right away if you saw Him." But no one knew where Jesus was.

Flash Card 5.2

4. Jesus Is Found in the Temple (vv. 46–47)

Joseph and Mary finally arrived in Jerusalem. Where would they look for Jesus now? Should they check the shops to see if He was looking at the items for sale? No. Jesus' parents knew Jesus wouldn't be shopping, since He hadn't asked them for permission. Should they check the streets and the parks to see if He was hanging out with other boys? No. Jesus' parents knew Jesus never spent time with boys His parents hadn't first approved of. Should they check the beautiful old buildings to see if He was looking at the amazing architecture? No. They knew there was nowhere Jesus would go without having first asked for their permission.

"Let's think…the last place either of us saw Jesus," Joseph said in a tired voice, "was in the temple. Let's go to the temple and see if anyone there remembers Him. Maybe someone can give us a clue as to where He may have gone."

"There have been so many boys who have come and gone this week—it would be a miracle if anyone remembered Jesus in particular," said Mary. But, still, she hadn't given up hope, and they went to the temple.

It had been three long days since they had left Jerusalem, and Mary and Joseph were tired and discouraged as they entered the temple. "I wonder who we should ask," began Joseph. But before all the words came out of His mouth, both he and Mary spied a group of Jewish teachers, called rabbis, and Jesus was right there in the middle of all of them!

Jesus was listening to the rabbis teach, and He was asking them questions about what they had taught. Then, the rabbis would ask Jesus questions to see if He understood what they had said, and these great teachers were "astonished at his understanding and answers" (v. 47). The rabbis had never before seen a twelve-year-old boy who knew so much about the Bible. They couldn't believe how much Jesus understood about God. They were amazed at how much Jesus wanted to learn. It seemed that He wanted to learn about God more than He wanted to do anything else in the world!

5. Mary Questions Jesus (v. 48)

Mary and Joseph were amazed to see Jesus there. They couldn't believe their eyes! They had been searching for Him for three long days, and now, here He was—in the temple where they had left Him. "Son, why have you done this to us?" His mother asked, her voice choked with crying. "Look at us—Your father and me. We have looked for You for three days, thinking something awful had happened to You, disappointed with ourselves that we hadn't looked after You better. Why, Jesus, why did You hurt us like this?"

Flash Card 5.3

6. Jesus' Business (vv. 49–50)

Jesus gently looked at His mother, then at Joseph, then back at His mother again. "Why did you worry? Why did you go through all this trouble looking for me? Didn't you know that my true Father is God in Heaven, and 'I must be about my Father's business?' (v. 49). My Father has a purpose for Me, and that is what I must do."

Mary and Joseph didn't understand what Jesus meant. But deep in their hearts they knew that Jesus was right. They knew that His true Father was God. They knew that Jesus had never, in His whole life, done anything wrong, and they knew He hadn't done wrong this time, either. They believed Him, and they returned to Nazareth.

7. Back Home in Nazareth (vv. 51–52)

When Joseph, Mary, and Jesus returned to their home in Nazareth, everything was the same as before. Jesus obeyed His parents, just as He had always obeyed them. Jesus was kind to His brothers and sisters, just as He had always been kind to them. Jesus worked hard in Joseph's carpentry shop, just as He had always worked. Jesus spoke respectfully, just as He had always spoken. Jesus told the truth, just as He had always told the truth. Jesus studied God's Word, just as He had always studied it. Yes, everything was the same.

But everything was different, too—at least in Mary's heart. Mary thought about what had happened on the Passover trip to Jerusalem. She thought about worrying where Jesus was. She thought about the sorrow she had when she was afraid of losing Him. She thought about finding Him in the temple with the Jewish teachers. She thought of how astonished the teachers were with Jesus' understanding. And she thought about Jesus saying, "I must be about my Father's business." As Mary thought about all these things, she realized that Jesus was very, very special.

And, although Jesus was the same, and He always will be the same, He grew. "And Jesus increased in wisdom and stature, and in favour with God and man" (Luke 2:52).

Hebrews 13:8

8   *Jesus Christ the same yesterday, and to day, and for ever.*

- He grew in understanding and wisdom. He had already known so much about God and about life, but He learned even more as time went on.
- Jesus' body grew, too. His muscles became large as He worked in the carpenter's shop with Joseph, and He grew tall. Jesus used His strength to serve God, His parents, and the people around Him.
- Jesus grew in the hearts of the people around Him. He served them and pleased them, and they thought very highly of Him. Not only did Jesus please the people around Him, but He grew to please God more and more. He always did what God wanted.

John 8:29b

29b for I do always those things that please him.

Jesus was the same as He had always been. He had always obeyed God and His parents. He had always made the right choices and done the right things. But even though He was the same, He grew.

APPLYING THE STORY

Jesus, in today's story, was twelve years old, and God didn't tell us very much about Jesus from the time He was a baby until now. God did, however, give us one very important verse that tells about Jesus before His twelfth birthday: "And the child grew, and waxed strong in spirit, filled with wisdom: and the grace of God was upon him" (Luke 2:40).

We know from this verse that, as a child, Jesus' body grew, just as you grow. Jesus got taller, and His muscles became stronger. We also know that His spirit grew strong. Jesus loved God, thought about and obeyed God, and made the right decisions; and that made His spirit—the part of a person who knows and worships God—grow stronger.

Teacher's Note

Wisdom: the right use or exercise of knowledge. Godly wisdom is the ability and desire to think and act according to Bible principles.

Romans 8:6

6 For to be carnally minded is death; but to be spiritually minded is life and peace.

We know that His mind and heart grew in wisdom. Jesus was filled with wisdom, and that tells us that He knew God the Father.

Teacher's Note

Fear of the Lord: belief that God is who He says He is; reverence and awe toward God; practicing His presence in your life.

Proverbs 9:10

10 *The fear of the LORD is the beginning of wisdom: and the knowledge of the holy is understanding.*

We know that the grace of God was upon Jesus. This means Jesus walked with His Father, and it showed up in the way He lived, the way He treated people, and the choices He made.

So, even before the story of the Passover trip to Jerusalem—before Jesus was twelve years old—the Bible tells us that Jesus grew in His body and His Spirit, and that God's grace was upon Him. And now, after the trip to Jerusalem, we see that Jesus continued to grow and that He pleased God and man. Jesus was successful both to God and people!

Isn't it wonderful that God told us in Luke 2 what Jesus was like as a child and as a teenager? Since we know what Jesus was like, we can do the things He did in order to be like Him.

The Bible tells us what pleases both God and man, and these are the things Jesus did.

Proverbs 3:1–4

1 *My son, forget not my law: but let thine heart keep my commandments:*

2 *For length of days, and long life, and peace, shall they add to thee.*

3 *Let not mercy and truth forsake thee: bind them about thy neck; write them upon the table of thine heart:*

4 *So shalt thou find favour and good understanding in the sight of God and man.*

- Jesus loved God's Word. (Law)
- Jesus obeyed God and His parents. (Commandments)
- Jesus was merciful. (Mercy)
- Jesus loved and told the truth. (Truth)

1 Timothy 4:12

12 *Let no man despise thy youth; but be thou an example of the believers, in word, in conversation, in charity, in spirit, in faith, in purity.*

- Jesus spoke with love, kindness, and grace. (Word)
- Jesus had good manners and chose to do the right things. (Conversation)
- Jesus was loving. (Charity)
- Jesus had a good disposition, or attitude. (Spirit)
- Jesus trusted and believed God. (Faith)
- Jesus had a pure mind and body. (Purity)

Jesus tells us in God's Word how we can grow as Jesus did.

- Ask God for wisdom, and learn from people who have God's wisdom.
- Read and obey the Bible—God's Word.
- Obey and honor God and our parents.
- Yield our tongues to the Lord so we speak lovingly, kindly, and truthfully.
- Learn and use good manners and show respect to all people.
- Ask God to give us love for others.
- Choose to be happy. Smile at people. Let Jesus give you joy.
- Always believe God. Trust Him to take care of you.
- Keep your mind pure by not looking at or thinking about things that don't please God.

Teacher's Note

Purity: freedom from guilt or the defilement of sin; innocence

The greatest goal you can have after you are saved is to be like Jesus, and today we have learned many qualities Jesus had as a child. Let's bow our heads and close our eyes and make a commitment in our hearts to the Lord that we are going to follow in the steps of Jesus and choose what Jesus chose when He was a child. (Pray.)

Review Game/Questions

Looking for Jesus

Materials Needed
Visuals for the Temple review game from the Ministry Resource CD.

Set up
Print visuals for the Temple review game. Print the Temple graphic on one side of cardstock and then print the points (Jesus) on the other side. Cut out cards. Laminate for durability. Place cards in a pocket chart or lay them on table (similar to the game show, Jeopardy).

Say to class, "Joseph and Mary were so excited to find Jesus at the Temple. In today's game the object is to find Jesus at the Temple."

Divide the class into teams. Call on a student from Team 1 to answer a question. If that student answers correctly, he may choose a card from the board by calling the color and amount of points. For example, "Blue for 100 points." If behind the temple you find the word "Jesus," your team receives the points listed on the front of the card. If behind the temple you find it blank, no points are awarded. Continue with Team 2. The team with the most points wins the game.

1. How old was Jesus in today's story?
   Answer: Twelve years old

2. What holiday were Jesus and His family celebrating?
   Answer: The Passover

3. Describe the trip back to Nazareth.
   Answer: Everyone was very happy and had a good time talking and fellowshipping in groups (of men, women, and children).

4. What did Joseph and Mary realize on the first night of their trip home?
   Answer: Jesus was not with them!

5. What did Joseph and Mary do once they realized they had left Jesus in Jerusalem?
   Answer: They went back to get Him.

6. Where did Mary and Joseph find Jesus?
   Answer: In the temple

7. What was Jesus doing in the temple?
    Answer: Listening to the rabbis teach and asking them questions

8. Did Jesus ever do anything wrong in His whole life?
    Answer: No!

9. In what four ways did Jesus grow?
    Answer: Wisdom, stature, favor with God, and favor with man.

10. How can you grow, like Jesus did?
    Answer: Answers will vary but might include examples listed on page 83.

 # Teaching the Memory Verse

Luke 2:52

52 And Jesus increased in wisdom and stature, and in favour with God and man.

Materials needed: 30 (9–11 inch) balloons (15 of each color)

Print two copies of Luke 2:52. Cut into word strips. Roll up each word and place inside a deflated balloon. Blow up balloons and knot end.

Together as a class, read Luke 2:52.

Babies are so cute! But it's not cute if they don't grow. In fact every time I took one of my children to the doctor, they would weigh them and measure them to make sure they were growing. It's one of the signs of a healthy child.

The Bible tells us that Jesus also grew! Because Jesus is God, His development was perfect and it was balanced. He grew in "wisdom and stature and in favour with God and man." We need to grow in those areas, too. Remember, a sign of a healthy Christian is to see spiritual growth!

Read the verse together again—several times, each time increasing the volume.

Divide the class into two teams, one team for each balloon color.

Have each team pop their own color balloons. Have them collect the word strips and then place the word strips in the correct verse order on the board. The team to finish this task first wins!

Object Lesson—Gone Missing

Materials Needed:

2" x 2" cards with consecutive numbers on each card to equal the number of children in your class.

Lesson:

Hand out a number to each child in your class on a 2" x 2" card. The numbers should be in consecutive order. Before class hide the number one card somewhere in the classroom that would be fairly easy for the class to find.

Have the class work together to put the numbers in order on the floor to find which number is missing.

When it is discovered that the number one card is missing, have the class search for the missing card. When the card has been found, regain the attention of the class.

Ask the children to describe what it felt like to discover one of the numbers missing. Ask the child who found the missing number to explain how he felt when he found the missing number.

Joseph and Mary could not find Jesus for three days. They looked everywhere for Him. When they found Jesus, He was sitting in the temple with the rabbis and talking with them. Joseph and Mary were probably very fearful something had happened to Jesus, but Jesus told them, "Did you not know that I must be about My Father's business?"

Craft—Scroll

Luke 2:52
And Jesus increased in wisdom and stature, and in favour with God and man.

Getting It Together

Paper
Wooden dowels

Per student:
2   Dowels
1   Piece of paper
1   Memory verse template located on the Ministry Resource CD

Putting It Together

1.   Print out a copy of the verse Luke 2:52 for each student.
2.   Instruct each child to glue one dowel on the right side of the paper and one on the left side of the paper.
3.   Roll each dowel toward the center of the paper.

Seeing It Together

Each student can have a real relationship with Jesus. They can grow and serve Him—even now. During craft time, discuss ideas that each student can do now to serve Jesus! (Telling someone about Jesus, obeying mom and dad at home, helping someone at church, cleaning up the classroom after church, etc.)

Additional Resources

Find the following items on the Ministry Resource CD:

•   Coloring Page (for younger children)

•   Activity Page (for older children)

•   Student Take-Home Paper

•   PowerPoint Presentation

Suggested Classroom Schedule

Before Class	Complete attendance record. Provide students with coloring pages/activity pages.
Opening	Welcome
Prayer	Prayer requests and praise reports from the children
Song Time	
Memory Verse	Matthew 3:17
Song Time	
Object Lesson	Identification
Bible Lesson	Jesus Is Baptized by John
Application/Invitation	Help saved students apply lesson. Invite unsaved students to receive Christ.
Snack	Jello Cups
Review Game/ Questions	Snowball Fight
Craft	Water & Dove Puzzle
Closing	Give announcements and pray. Distribute take-home papers.

Lesson Six Overview

Jesus Is Baptized by John

Theme—Baptism identifies us with Jesus.

Scripture
Matthew 3:13–17

Memory Verse
Matthew 3:17—"And lo a voice from heaven, saying, This is my beloved Son, in whom I am well pleased."

Lesson Outline

Introducing the Story
Have you ever seen someone get baptized? Today we are going to learn about when Jesus was baptized.

Telling the Story

1. **John the Baptist Baptizes in the Jordan River**
   (vv. 1–12)

2. **Jesus Comes from Galilee to be Baptized by John**
   (v. 13, Luke 3:23a, Luke 3:21)—Flash Card 6.1

3. **Jesus Answers John's Objection** (v. 15,
   Philippians 2:7–8)—Flash Card 6.2

4. **The Trinity Is Seen in the Baptism of Jesus** (vv. 16–17,
   Luke 3:21, John 1:32–34, Isaiah 42:1, John 8:29b)
   —Flash Card 6.3

Applying the Story (1 Corinthians 1:17a, Hebrews 9:22b,
Matthew 28:19, 3:13, Acts 2:41)
The Bible teaches that baptism is a symbol—a picture—of what has happened on the inside of a person. God wants every Christian to be baptized to show other people that he or she has trusted Jesus.

6 Lesson Six

Jesus Is Baptized by John

Theme: Baptism identifies us with Jesus.

Scripture

Matthew 3:13–17

13 *Then cometh Jesus from Galilee to Jordan unto John, to be baptized of him.*

14 *But John forbad him, saying, I have need to be baptized of thee, and comest thou to me?*

15 *And Jesus answering said unto him, Suffer it to be so now: for thus it becometh us to fulfil all righteousness. Then he suffered him.*

16 *And Jesus, when he was baptized, went up straightway out of the water: and, lo, the heavens were opened unto him, and he saw the Spirit of God descending like a dove, and lighting upon him:*

17 *And lo a voice from heaven, saying, This is my beloved Son, in whom I am well pleased.*

Memory Verse

Matthew 3:17
"And lo a voice from heaven, saying, This is my beloved Son, in whom I am well pleased."

Snack Suggestion

Jello Cups
Prepare blue Jello in individual clear cups for children to enjoy after the lesson. After a child accepts Jesus as Saviour, the child can identify with Christ in baptism.

Teacher's Note

Before teaching this lesson, be sure you are familiar with your church policies for baptizing children. When talking with children about baptism, let them know they will need their parent's permission, and offer to visit their homes to talk to their parents about salvation and baptism. If your church requires written permission of the parents, be prepared to explain this to the parents and bring a written permission slip for them to sign if this is your church's procedure.

✓ Teacher's Checklist

- ❑ Read Matthew 3:13–17 daily.
- ❑ Study Lesson Six.
- ❑ Flash cards 6.1—6.3
- ❑ Gather for lesson—wedding ring, piece of paper.
- ❑ Prepare snack—Jello Cups.
- ❑ Gather for object lesson—name tags, black marker.
- ❑ Gather supplies for review game—magnet or Velcro.
- ❑ Print visuals for review game.
- ❑ Print memory verse images from the Ministry Resource CD.
- ❑ Print for craft—puzzle.
- ❑ Gather for craft—crayons, paper, and scissors.
- ❑ Print and duplicate Coloring Pages or Activity Pages on the Ministry Resource CD (one per student).
- ❑ Print and duplicate Take-Home Paper on the Ministry Resource CD (one per student).

Bible Lesson

Scripture: Matthew 3:13–17

INTRODUCING THE STORY

Have you ever seen someone get baptized? (Allow students to answer.) Who did you see get baptized? Who baptized him or her? How was he or she baptized? (Be prepared for varied responses that will likely include infant baptism.) Ask questions that encourage the students to tell you everything they saw during the baptisms at which they were present. Later in the lesson you will explain the meaning and procedures for biblical baptism, but for now, just listen to your students' descriptions and interpretations of the baptisms they have viewed.

Today we are going to learn about when Jesus was baptized.

THE STORY

1. John the Baptist Baptizes in the Jordan River (vv. 1–12)

John the Baptist was Jesus' cousin, whom we learned about in our first lesson in our study of the life of Jesus. John's parents, Zacharias and Elisabeth, were very old when John was born—too old, in fact, to have children. But God performed a miracle and allowed them to have a baby when they were past the time of life when people have babies.

When God performs a miracle, it is because He has a very important plan He intends to accomplish through that miracle. That's the way it was with John the Baptist. God had a very special plan for John's life. Does anyone remember what that plan was? (John the Baptist was going to be the last prophet to tell the Jews that their promised Saviour—Jesus Christ— was coming. He was also going to be the very special preacher who would tell people that the Saviour was finally here, and that they needed to trust Him.) That is exactly what John was doing in our Bible story today.

Now, you have to understand, John didn't fully know that Jesus was the promised Saviour. So, when he preached, he didn't tell everyone, "You need to trust Jesus." He said, "You need to trust the one who is the Saviour. God has sent Him to the world, and you need Him to forgive your sins."

Teaching Tip

Tell your students that we call our lessons Bible stories because they are stories God told us in the Bible. Sometimes we think of stories as being make-believe, and many stories *are* made up, but the wonderful thing about stories in the Bible is that they are all true—everything in the Bible is true!

You may have a picture in your mind of how the very special preacher, John the Baptist, looked. You might picture him looking something like our pastor. Maybe you imagine him looking very sharp, in a nice suit with a tie, standing behind a pulpit—like our pastor. (Describe your own pastor in this paragraph.)

The Bible gives us quite a different picture of John the Baptist. As a child, he grew up in the desert, and he learned to live very simply. He gathered wild honey and locusts for his meals. His clothing was made of a plain, rough fabric woven from camel's hair, and a leather belt held his robe together. John the Baptist wasn't at all fancy. Just as he grew up in the wilderness of the desert, he also preached and baptized in the wilderness.

So, there was John the Baptist, a strong, roughly dressed preacher, telling people that Jesus was here, and that they needed to repent and come to Jesus. "Hundreds of years ago," cried John, "the prophet Isaiah said I would be here, telling the world to turn from their sins to the Saviour. And now I am doing just as Isaiah said I would do. Repent—turn to the Saviour! Trust Him!"

Many people went into the wilderness to listen to John preach, and many of them believed John's message, repented, and were baptized.

Flash Card 6.1

2. Jesus Comes from Galilee to be Baptized by John (v. 13)

The day was very busy—many people had believed John's message and asked John to baptize them. By being baptized of John, they were identifying with his message and outwardly expressing their heart decision to trust the Saviour. John had great joy in his heart as he saw so many people turn from their sins to the Saviour. He gladly baptized them—one by one.

A man came down into the river with John. "I am turning from my sin to the Saviour," he told John, "and I would like to be baptized."

"Wonderful!" John almost shouted for joy. And he baptized the man.

A woman came into the river with John. "I am so sorry I have lived for myself, trying to do things my own way, and I have not trusted in the Saviour. I am trusting Him today, and I want to be baptized."

John gladly baptized the woman.

There were many people who came to be baptized that day. John stood in the water of the Jordan River, and as each person came for baptism, he called them to come down into the water with him. Then, John would place

> ## ✎ Teacher's Note
>
> **Repent**: to change one's mind; to turn around; to change direction; to turn from unbelief to belief

his hand behind the person's neck and lower him or her back into the water, just as God had told him to do.

After the last person had been baptized that day, one more man came forward to be baptized—a man about thirty years of age.

> **Luke 3:23a**
>
> *23a And Jesus himself began to be about thirty years of age*

> **Luke 3:21**
>
> *21   Now when all the people were baptized, it came to pass, that Jesus also being baptized and praying, the heaven was opened.*

Jesus stepped to the edge of the river, and said, "John, I would like to be baptized." No one really knew Jesus yet—no one knew that He was the Saviour about whom John had been preaching. But since it was so out of the ordinary for someone to step forward after John had already finished baptizing, everyone knew something very unusual was about to happen. And they all watched to see what it would be.

John looked in amazement at Jesus and said, "I have need to be baptized of thee, and comest thou to me?" John knew that Jesus should be baptizing him. "I can't baptize You. I am not worthy," said John.

> **✎ Teacher's Note**
>
> **Baptism**: to plunge or to dunk.
> The Bible teaches that you should be baptized in water by immersion rather than sprinkling. Because baptism is a picture of Christ's death, burial, and resurrection, only immersion correctly pictures this.
> For more information, refer to the brochure, "Baptism—My Outward Expression of My Inward Decision" available from Striving Together Publications.

3. Jesus Answers John's Objection (v. 15)

Flash Card 6.2

Jesus spoke loudly to John so that everyone else would be able to hear. "The reason I need to be baptized," Jesus said, "is because it is God's plan. The right thing for Me to do is to do everything God has planned for His followers to do; everything He has told us to do—everything."

Jesus knew that, although He was God, He was also a man; and as a man, the Father's purpose for His life was for Him to do everything God required of men. God wanted people to see that Jesus had to be born, just like they were born. God wanted people to see that He had to grow, just like they did. God wanted people to see that in obedience to God, Jesus had to be baptized, just like they did.

Jesus, who was God, chose to become a man so He could pay the price for the sin of every person.

Philippians 2:7–8

7 But made himself of no reputation, and took upon him the form of a servant, and was made in the likeness of men:

8 And being found in fashion as a man, he humbled himself, and became obedient unto death, even the death of the cross.

And so, John the Baptist, who trusted Jesus and knew everything Jesus did and said was right, baptized the Lord Jesus Christ.

Flash Card 6.3

4. The Trinity Is Seen in the Baptism of Jesus (vv. 16–17)

As Jesus came back up out of the water, He prayed to the Father.

Luke 3:21

21 Now when all the people were baptized, it came to pass, that Jesus also being baptized, and praying, the heaven was opened.

And immediately, everything was different! The heavens opened to Jesus, (can you imagine what it was like to see the heavens open up?) and the Holy Spirit of God came to Jesus. We can't usually see the Holy Spirit, but that day, at that moment, the Holy Spirit looked like a dove.

Then, the most beautiful voice spoke from Heaven—the voice of God the Father! "This is My beloved Son, in whom I am well pleased." And all at once, everyone knew that God the Father in Heaven was saying that Jesus was God the Son. They knew then and there that the Father said that Jesus was the Messiah, the Saviour that had come to pay for their sins.

It was at that moment that John the Baptist also knew for certain that Jesus was the Saviour of the world, the Son of God.

John 1:32–34

32 And John bare record, saying, I saw the Spirit descending from heaven like a dove, and it abode upon him.

33   *And I knew him not: but he that sent me to baptize with*
     water, the same said unto me, Upon whom thou shalt see
     the Spirit descending, and remaining on him, the same is he
     which baptizeth with the Holy Ghost.
34   *And I saw, and bare record that this is the Son of God.*

Can you imagine how happy Jesus was to hear God the Father say that He was well pleased with Him—that He delighted in Him?

Isaiah 42:1
1   *Behold my servant, whom I uphold; mine elect, in whom*
    my soul delighteth; I have put my spirit upon him: he shall
    bring forth judgment to the Gentiles.

When Jesus was baptized, He was doing exactly what God the Father wanted Him to do, just as He always did.

John 8:29b
29b *for I do always those things that please him.*

Teaching Tip

This passage lends itself to a teaching on the Trinity, as all three parts of the Trinity are seen together at Jesus' baptism:

- God the Father speaking from Heaven
- The Son on Earth being baptized
- The Holy Spirit descending in the form of a dove

APPLYING THE STORY

The Bible teaches that baptism is a symbol—a picture—of what has happened on the inside of a person. God wants every Christian (a Christian is someone who has trusted Jesus as his or her Saviour from sin) to be baptized to show other people that he or she has trusted Jesus.

When a person is baptized, it is a picture of what Jesus did for us. When he goes under the water, it is a picture of when Jesus died and was buried. And when he comes back up from the water, it pictures how Jesus rose from the dead. When someone is baptized, it is like he is saying to everyone, "See, I want you to know that I trusted in Jesus—that He died for my sins and rose from the dead. Now, I want everyone to know that I belong to Him and that I want to live for Him!"

Some people believe that baptism washes away sins, but that is not what the Bible teaches. The Bible says that the only way for sins to be forgiven, or washed away, is by trusting in the blood Jesus shed when He died on the cross. Baptism, or anything other than Jesus' blood, won't take away our sins. It is only through trusting in Jesus as Saviour that a person is saved from his or her sin.

1 Corinthians 1:17a

17a For Christ sent me not to baptize, but to preach the gospel:

Hebrews 9:22b

22b without shedding of blood is no remission.

Teaching Tip

Show the children your own wedding ring or a picture of a wedding ring.

Think about two people getting married. They give each other wedding rings. Do the wedding rings they give each other make them married? (No, a wedding ring shows people that a man and woman are married.) Does baptism save a person from his sins? (No, baptism shows people that a person has trusted Jesus to save him from his sins.) Just like a wedding ring shows people that a man and woman are husband and wife, baptism shows people that a person has trusted in Jesus.

If the purpose for baptism were to wash away sins, the Father wouldn't have wanted Jesus to be baptized, because Jesus never sinned. He didn't have any sins that needed to be washed away.

The Bible tells us that a person is to be baptized only after he has trusted Jesus as his Saviour, and the Bible gives three reasons we should be baptized:

God commands it.

Matthew 28:19

19 Go ye therefore, and teach all nations, baptizing them in the name of the Father, and of the Son, and of the Holy Ghost.

Christ was our example.

Matthew 3:13

13 Then cometh Jesus from Galilee to Jordan unto John, to be baptized of him.

Believers in the Bible practiced it.

Acts 2:41

41 Then they that gladly received his word were baptized.

Jesus was baptized to show that He was the Saviour of the world, the Son of God, and He always did what pleased the Father.

Baptism is like an announcement to the world that you have trusted Jesus to be your Saviour. When we are baptized, it is telling everyone that we are Christians, and we want them to know it.

We who are Christians are to be baptized to show that we trust Jesus as our Saviour and we want to obey God in everything, just as Jesus did.

Maybe you have never trusted Jesus as your Saviour. Maybe you are like the people that John the Baptist preached to who needed to first put their faith in Jesus. Remember, there is nothing we do to earn being God's child or going to Heaven. Even baptism doesn't make you saved. You need to choose to trust Jesus first.

Have you ever been saved? If you don't remember for sure or if in your heart right now you have a question about it, please talk to me after class. I would like to explain more about it to you and help you trust Jesus.

Maybe you have already been saved, but you have never been baptized the way Jesus showed us we should be baptized. If you are saved and would like to be baptized, I would like to talk to you after class as well.

Or maybe, you have been saved and baptized. That's wonderful! Remember, that baptism is a way of telling everyone that you are a Christian and you want them to know it. Are you living all throughout the week so people would know you are a Christian? Just like you obeyed Jesus and followed His example to be baptized, you want to obey and follow His example in the way you obey your parents and teachers, treat your brothers and sisters, and show kindness to others.

When you think about baptism or when you see someone get baptized, remember that it is the way God designed for someone who is saved to show others that they trusted Jesus and are happy for everyone else to know that He is their Saviour!

Act It Out

Roll up a piece of paper in a cone shape to look like a megaphone. Hold it up to your mouth as you make your "announcement" that you have been saved. This would be a good place for you to share your personal testimony of salvation and baptism. Tell your students that getting baptized is a way of sharing with others the good news that you have been saved.

Review Game/Questions

Snowball Fight

Materials Needed

Visuals for Snowball Fight from the Ministry Resource CD.

Set up

Print visuals for Snowball Fight from the Ministry Resource CD. Cut out the visuals and place a magnet (or Velcro) on the back of each piece, so it will adhere to the board. In class, put a snowman on each side of the board, along with an equal amount of non-numbered snowballs. Place the numbered snowballs into a bag.

Playing the Game

Divide the class into two teams. Ask a question from today's lesson. The student who answers the question may pull out a snowball containing a number from the bag. Then that student may take that same amount of snowballs and "throw" them at the other team (just move the snowball to the other team's pile). Whichever team runs out of snowballs first wins the game. (Or the team with the least amount of snowballs wins the game.)

1. How were Jesus and John the Baptist related?
   Answer: They were cousins.

2. What did John the Baptist eat?
   Answer: Wild honey and locusts

3. What did John the Baptist wear?
   Answer: A robe made of camel's hair

4. What message did John the Baptist preach?
   Answer: Trust the one who is Saviour to be forgiven of your sins!

5. What did the people do after they made the heart decision to believe in the Saviour?
   Answer: They were baptized.

6. Where did John the Baptist baptize?
   Answer: In the Jordan River

7. At first, did John want to baptize Jesus? Why or why not?
   Answer: No, he didn't, because he didn't think he was worthy.

8. What happened after Jesus was baptized?
   Answer: The heavens opened.

9. What did the voice from Heaven say?
   Answer: "This is my beloved Son, in whom I am well pleased."

10. Why was God, the Heavenly Father, pleased with His Son, Jesus?
    Answer: Because He obeyed God and followed His plan.

 # Teaching the Memory Verse

Matthew 3:17

17 And lo a voice from heaven, saying, This is my beloved Son, in whom I am well pleased.

Echo, Echo, Echo
Divide the class into three sections. Instruct the students to repeat after you, as an echo. The first section will repeat loudly, then gradually decrease the volume with each section.
Teacher says… "And lo…"
Section #1—they echo in a loud voice: "And lo…"
Section #2—they echo in a quiet (or regular) voice: "And lo…"
Section #3—they echo in a whisper: "And lo…"

Continue in the same manner with the next phrases
- a voice from heaven,
- saying,
- This is my beloved Son,
- In whom I am well pleased.
- Matthew 3:17

Do this again, but this time the teacher doesn't say anything, simply point to Section 1 to begin the echos.
   Use companion flash cards found in Visual Resource Packet or images found on the Ministry Resource CD.

Object Lesson—Identification

Materials Needed:
Name tags
Black marker

Lesson:
When the children arrive to class, give them name tags and have them write their names on the tags and stick them on the front of themselves. Once all the children are seated, ask each child what his names is. After everyone has said his name, ask another child to say the name of the person beside him. Ask all the children, "Why do you wear a name tag? Is it because you don't know your own name? No, it is to let others know what your name is. The name tag is there to let everyone else know what your parents named you!"

Baptism is a command to let everyone in the church know that you have trusted Christ as your Saviour. It is an outward picture of an inward decision and identifies you as a believer of Jesus Christ.

Additional Resources

Find the following items on the Ministry Resource CD:

- Coloring Page (for younger children)
- Activity Page (for older children)
- Student Take-Home Paper
- PowerPoint Presentation

Craft—Water & Dove Puzzle

Getting It Together

Crayons
Paper
Scissors

Per student:
1   Puzzle template from the Ministry
    Resource CD

Putting It Together

1.   Print out the puzzle on cardstock.
2.   Color the puzzle.
3.   Cut the pieces out.

Seeing It Together

After a student asks Jesus to be his personal Saviour, he can follow in baptism. It is the first step in the Christian life and is a picture showing people of the decision to trust Christ as Saviour. (Remember that baptism does not take you to heaven.)

Jesus was baptized as an example to each of us. He was a wonderful example!

Suggested Classroom Schedule

Before Class	Complete attendance record. Provide students with coloring pages/activity pages.
Opening	Welcome
Prayer	Prayer requests and praise reports from the children
Song Time	
Memory Verse	James 4:7
Song Time	
Object Lesson	Tempted
Bible Lesson	Jesus Defeats Temptation
Application/Invitation	Help saved students apply lesson. Invite unsaved students to receive Christ.
Snack	Animal Cookies
Review Game/Questions	Roaring Lion!
Craft	Puppet
Closing	Give announcements and pray. Distribute take-home papers.

Lesson Seven Overview

Jesus Defeats Temptation

Theme—Jesus can help us defeat the devil.

Scripture
Luke 4:1–14

Memory Verse
James 4:7— *"Submit yourselves therefore to God. Resist the devil, and he will flee from you."*

Lesson Outline

Introducing the Story

In our Bible story today, we are going to learn about when the devil tempted Jesus, and what Jesus did when He was tempted. Listen closely, because you will learn from Jesus how to resist temptation.

Telling the Story

1. **Jesus Is Led by the Spirit into the Wilderness** (v.1, John 8:29b, Matthew 3:1, Mark 1:13a)

2. **Jesus Fasted and Was Tempted for Forty Days** (v. 2)

3. **The Devil Tempts Jesus with Bread** (v.3)—*Flash Card 7.1*

4. **Jesus Answers the Devil's Temptation with Scripture** (v. 4, James 4:8, Psalm 119:11, Deuteronomy 8:3)

5. **The Devil Tempts Jesus with Power** (vv. 5–7)—*Flash Card 7.2*

6. **Jesus Answers the Devil's Temptation with Scripture** (v. 8, Deuteronomy 6:13)

7. **The Devil Tempts Jesus to Show His Power** (vv. 9–11, Psalm 91:11–12)—*Flash Card 7.3*

8. **Jesus Answers the Devil's Temptation with Scripture** (v.12, Deuteronomy 6:16)

9. **The Devil Leaves Jesus for a Time** (v. 13)

Applying the Story

You will face many temptations throughout your life. God gives us all we need to resist temptation, and He gives us all we need to pick us up when we fall.

7 Lesson Seven

Jesus Defeats Temptation

Theme: Jesus can help us defeat the devil.

 ## Scripture

Luke 4:1–14

1 And Jesus being full of the Holy Ghost returned from Jordan, and was led by the Spirit into the wilderness,

2 Being forty days tempted of the devil. And in those days he did eat nothing: and when they were ended, he afterward hungered.

3 And the devil said unto him, If thou be the Son of God, command this stone that it be made bread.

4 And Jesus answered him, saying, It is written, That man shall not live by bread alone, but by every word of God.

5 And the devil, taking him up into an high mountain, shewed unto him all the kingdoms of the world in a moment of time.

6 And the devil said unto him, All this power will I give thee, and the glory of them: for that is delivered unto me; and to whomsoever I will I give it.

7 If thou therefore wilt worship me, all shall be thine.

8 And Jesus answered and said unto him, Get thee behind me, Satan: for it is written, Thou shalt worship the Lord thy God, and him only shalt thou serve.

9 And he brought him to Jerusalem, and set him on a pinnacle of the temple, and said unto him, If thou be the Son of God, cast thyself down from hence:

10 For it is written, He shall give his angels charge over thee, to keep thee:

11 And in their hands they shall bear thee up, lest at any time thou dash thy foot against a stone.

12 And Jesus answering said unto him, It is said, Thou shalt not tempt the Lord thy God.

13 And when the devil had ended all the temptation, he departed from him for a season.

14 And Jesus returned in the power of the Spirit into Galilee: and there went out a fame of him through all the region round about.

Teacher's Checklist

 **Snack Suggestion**

Animal Cookies
Can you find the lion? The Bible says that the devil is as a lion, seeking whom he may devour. Just as Jesus used Scripture to defeat the devil, we need to hide God's Word in our hearts.

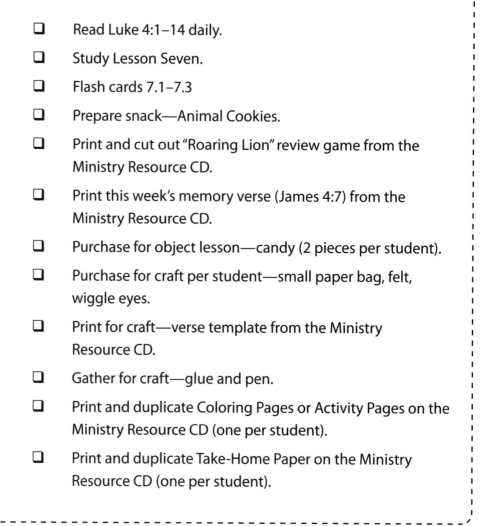

- ❑ Read Luke 4:1–14 daily.
- ❑ Study Lesson Seven.
- ❑ Flash cards 7.1–7.3
- ❑ Prepare snack—Animal Cookies.
- ❑ Print and cut out "Roaring Lion" review game from the Ministry Resource CD.
- ❑ Print this week's memory verse (James 4:7) from the Ministry Resource CD.
- ❑ Purchase for object lesson—candy (2 pieces per student).
- ❑ Purchase for craft per student—small paper bag, felt, wiggle eyes.
- ❑ Print for craft—verse template from the Ministry Resource CD.
- ❑ Gather for craft—glue and pen.
- ❑ Print and duplicate Coloring Pages or Activity Pages on the Ministry Resource CD (one per student).
- ❑ Print and duplicate Take-Home Paper on the Ministry Resource CD (one per student).

Bible Lesson

Scripture: Luke 4:1–14

INTRODUCING THE STORY

"Hey, Mom made cookies! I love cookies! Oh, they smell so good! I remember she said she was going to make cookies for the meeting tonight. I wonder if she would notice if I took just one or two? She almost always makes more than she needs, and I'm her daughter (or son)—she should make extra cookies for me. I'm going to take just two. I'd better take them to my room to eat them, so Mom doesn't come in and find me eating her cookies."

"Oh, it feels so good to get into bed! Aw, I forgot to brush my teeth. I know Dad and Mom want me to brush my teeth every night before I go to bed, but I'm so tired tonight. They won't even know that I didn't brush my teeth. I think I'll go to sleep just this once without brushing my teeth."

"Dad left change out on his dresser. I wonder if he knows how much is there. I doubt it—Dad has a lot of money. He doesn't need his change. But if I had that money, I could buy a soda or some gum. I'll just take seventy-five cents. He'll never even know."

Something happened to me in each of these little stories I just acted out. Do you know what it was? (I was tempted to do wrong, and I chose to "give in" to the temptation and do the wrong thing.)

Did I have to give in? Could I have resisted the temptation and done right? In our Bible story today, we are going to learn about when the devil tempted Jesus, and what Jesus did when He was tempted. Listen closely, because you will learn from Jesus how to resist temptation.

Act It Out

As you play-act these scenarios, make them seem real. Bring a cookie jar to class, and act out putting your hand into the cookie jar, taking it back out, putting it in again, etc. as you think about whether or not you should actually take a cookie.

Set a toothbrush and toothpaste in plain sight as a visual while you are deciding not to brush your teeth. Place a pile of change on the table or podium and count it as you go through the temptation with Dad's money.

THE STORY

1. Jesus Is Led by the Spirit into the Wilderness (v. 1)

The day had been so perfect. Jesus had just been baptized, and when He came out of the water, God the Holy Spirit showed Himself in the shape of a dove and landed on Jesus (God the Son); and the heavens opened, and God the Father had said the sweetest words Jesus heard while He was on earth, "This is my beloved Son, in whom I am well pleased." It was so wonderful to hear those words from His Father, because everything Jesus chose to do was for the purpose of pleasing His Father. And He was happy that He had pleased His Father.

John 8:29b

29b for I do always those things that please him.

Teaching Tip

The Spirit was not going to tempt Jesus, as "God cannot be tempted with evil, neither tempteth he any man," (James 1:13).

He was, rather, leading Him into the wilderness where Satan would tempt Him. Jesus' temptation allows us to understand that He is touched with the feeling of our weakness and allows us to be comforted by Him.

Hebrews 4:15—*For we have not an high priest which cannot be touched with the feeling of our infirmities; but was in all points tempted like as we are, yet without sin.*

Hebrews 2:18—*For in that he himself hath suffered being tempted, he is able to succour them that are tempted.*

As Jesus was leaving the Jordan River where He had been baptized, the Holy Spirit led Him to go deeper into the wilderness, and Jesus knew that the purpose of this trip was for Him to be tempted by the devil.

Matthew 3:1

1 Then was Jesus led up of the spirit into the wilderness to be tempted of the devil.

In the land of Judaea, where Jesus lived, the wilderness had hardly any plants—just scrubby bushes—and it was full of stones. Wild animals roamed in the wilderness, looking for food and water.

Mark 1:13a

13a And he was there in the wilderness forty days, tempted of Satan; and was with the wild beasts;

"If it were up to me," thought Jesus, "I wouldn't choose to come to this wilderness—and I don't want to be tempted by the devil. But, since God the Holy Spirit has led Me here, this is the best place for Me to be. I trust My Father to lead Me rightly, and I only want to please Him."

2. Jesus Fasted and Was Tempted for Forty Days (v. 2)

Jesus knew that He needed strength from God the Father in order to be able to resist the temptations with which the devil was going to tempt Him. "I need to be prepared for the temptations the devil is going to bring to Me, and one thing I know to do to help Me keep My focus on My Father is to fast."

So there, in the wilderness, Jesus spent forty days and forty nights, eating nothing, alone with His Father. The devil would come to Jesus and try to get Him to do wrong or to think wrong thoughts, but Jesus always resisted the temptation.

Finally, the forty days of fasting were finished, and Jesus was very hungry.

3. The Devil Tempts Jesus with Bread (v. 3)

Flash Card 7.1

"Jesus has to be very hungry now," thought the devil. "In fact, I believe He is almost starving. When a person is really hungry, he can be tempted to eat almost anything! Ha ha ha! This is the exact moment for me to bring a great temptation to Jesus—He won't be able to resist the temptation for food now! Not even Jesus could resist now!"

So, the devil came to Jesus and said, "If you really are the Son of God, as you say you are, why don't you command this stone that it be made into bread? I mean, if God really is your Father, and if you really are His Son, surely God wouldn't mind if you just take care of yourself. God knows everyone needs to eat. Come on, it's for your own good!"

4. Jesus Answers the Devil's Temptation with Scripture (v. 4)

At that moment, Jesus was glad He had followed God the Holy Spirit and had gone everywhere He told Him to go and had done everything He told Him to do. Jesus knew that at a time of great temptation like this, He needed to have the strength of the Holy Spirit helping Him and giving Him courage. He knew that if He submitted Himself to God, the Holy Spirit would help Him, and the devil would run from Him.

James 4:8

8   *Submit yourselves therefore to God. Resist the devil, and he will flee from you.*

Jesus was not only thankful He had submitted to the Holy Spirit, but He was also thankful He had read and memorized the Bible. He was thankful Mary and Joseph had taught Him God's Word, and that He had continued to learn it on His own after He was grown. Jesus knew God would use His Word to help Him defeat the devil and overcome temptation.

Teacher's Note

Fasting: to abstain from food beyond the usual time; to omit to take the usual meals for a time; voluntary abstinence from food to express grief or to pray against an expected evil

Tempt: to entice to do something wrong by presenting arguments that are convincing, or by the offer of some pleasure or apparent advantage

Resist: to stand against; to withstand; to act in opposition

Teacher's Note

Submit: to yield, resign, or surrender to the power, will, or authority of another; to be subject

Psalm 119:11

11   *Thy word have I hid in mine heart, that I might not sin*
     against thee.

Because Jesus had followed the leading of God the Holy Spirit, and because Jesus had hidden God's Word in His heart, He was able to answer the devil. "It is written in the Bible," Jesus said to the devil, "That man shall not live by bread alone, but by every word of God."

Deuteronomy 8:3

3   *And he humbled thee, and suffered thee to hunger, and*
    fed thee with manna, which thou knewest not, neither
    did thy fathers know; that he might make thee know that
    man doth not live by bread only, but by every word that
    proceedeth out of the mouth of the LORD doth man live.

"Bread isn't the most important thing in My life—not even now, when I am so hungry after not eating for forty days and forty nights. In fact, sometimes God allows us to be hungry so we can know that He is more important to us than food. The most important thing in My life," Jesus said to the devil, "is knowing and following God's Word. My Father gives Me everything I need, and I trust Him."

Flash Card 7.2

5. The Devil Tempts Jesus with Power (vv. 5–7)

"Well, that didn't work," thought Satan. "But I'm not going to give up so easily—I have another idea: If I can just get Him to sin, there won't be a perfect Saviour to save people from their sin, no one will be able to be saved, and I will be stronger than God!"

So, the devil took Jesus up to a high mountain, and showed Him all the kingdoms of the world. "Will you look at this?" the devil said. "Why, think of how beautiful all these kingdoms are. Think of all the money there—and you could have it all! Think of how people would admire you if you were the ruler of all these kingdoms. You could be the ruler of all of this," the devil tempted Jesus, "if you will just fall down and worship me. Just think how easy it would be—you could have control of all the world without having to go through all the pain the Father is going to put you through."

6. Jesus Answers the Devil's Temptation with Scripture (v. 8)

Jesus knew Satan's (the devil's) tricks. He knew Satan was only showing Him the good part—the exciting part—of the kingdoms of the world. The devil was trying to tempt Jesus with glory and power, but the devil didn't realize how much Jesus loved people. When Jesus looked at all those kingdoms, He knew that those kingdoms were full of sinful people who needed a Saviour. He knew that if He accepted Satan's temptation, He wouldn't be the perfect Saviour, and He couldn't pay for the sins of all the people in those kingdoms.

Jesus also knew that Satan's offers are lies—that Satan only shows us what he wants us to see. He doesn't show us the hard things that will happen to us if we fall to his temptations. He makes sin look like it will make us happy, when in the end, it will always bring us pain and sadness.

"My Father will take care of Me and provide everything I need," thought Jesus. "I will wait for Him to give Me what He wants for Me in His perfect time and His perfect way." Then, turning to the devil, Jesus commanded, "Get out of here, Satan."

Jesus was again glad He had followed God the Holy Spirit—going where He led Him and doing what He told Him to do. He was glad He had submitted Himself to the Father and had His strength to overcome temptation.

Jesus was also glad He knew the Scriptures. Again, He used the Word of God that He had hidden in His heart to defeat Satan. He said, "For it is written, Thou shalt worship the Lord thy God, and him only shalt thou serve."

Deuteronomy 6:13

13 *Thou shalt fear the LORD thy God, and serve him, and shalt swear by his name.*

"I will not be tricked by Satan, the liar, who would like Me to believe that what he can give Me is better than what My Father gives in His perfect time and His perfect way."

Flash Card 7.3

7. The Devil Tempts Jesus to Show His Power (vv. 9–11)

"I'm not going to give up yet," thought the devil. "What would be something that would really tempt Jesus? What problem does He have that I could give Him the answer to? I've got it! Jesus has come as the Messiah, but many people don't believe that He is the Messiah, the Saviour of the world. If I gave Him the opportunity to do some amazing miracle, He would think that would prove to everyone He is the Messiah they have been waiting for. Ha! That's it!"

So, Satan went to Jesus again, and he brought Him to Jerusalem and set Him on the very highest place at the top of the temple. "If you really are the Son of God," he tempted Jesus again, "throw yourself off this temple."

"Jesus has been quoting Scripture to resist temptation," thought the devil. "I will quote Scripture in order to tempt Him to sin. And, I will quote it incorrectly. I will twist it around to make it say what I want it to say."

Satan looked at Jesus and quoted the Bible, "He shall give his angels charge over thee, to keep thee: And in their hands they shall bear thee up, lest at any time thou dash thy foot against a stone."

Psalm 91:11–12

11 *For he shall give his angels charge over thee, to keep thee in all thy ways.*

12 *They shall bear thee up in their hands, lest thou dash thy foot against a stone.*

Satan said, "The Bible says the angels will take care of You, and they will hold You up so You won't even cut Your foot on a rock. Go ahead—throw Yourself down. Then everyone will know that You are God. You want them to believe you, don't You?"

Teacher's Note

The context of Psalm 91 is God's protection and care for those who abide in Him, not for those who go their own way, as Satan was tempting Jesus to do. Thus, Satan was twisting Scripture to fit his agenda.

8. Jesus Answers the Devil's Temptation with Scripture (v. 12)

For the third time, Jesus was thankful He had followed God the Holy Spirit. He was glad He had trusted Him to lead Him to go to the right place and to do the right thing. He knew the Spirit was giving Him strength right now.

Jesus was also glad He had memorized Scripture. He knew God would again use the Scripture He had learned to defeat the temptations Satan was throwing at Him.

Then and there Jesus remembered a story from the Old Testament. God's people, the Jews, had been wandering in the wilderness, and they became thirsty. "God isn't taking care of us," they complained. "We don't have water, and we don't think we can trust God or the leader He has given us any more."

God told Moses, their leader, to stand in front of a certain rock and to hit the rock with a stick. God said that when Moses did this, water would come out of the rock!

Moses believed God and did what God had said. And, of course, water came out of the rock, just as God had promised. But, God was not pleased with the people, because they complained and didn't trust Him. Moses was not pleased with the people, either, because they were tempting, or testing, God. They were tempting Him to prove that He was God by doing some miracle, when He just wanted them to trust Him.

As Jesus remembered that story, He also remembered what God had said about it later on in the Bible, and that is the Scripture that Jesus quoted to Satan. "Thou shalt not tempt the Lord thy God."

Deuteronomy 6:16

16 *Ye shall not tempt the Lord your God, as ye tempted him in Massah.*

"God is God," said Jesus. "He is always good, and He is always right, and He commands us not to ask Him to prove anything. We are only to trust Him."

9. The Devil Leaves Jesus for a Time (v. 13)

"Well, if Jesus didn't fall to that last temptation, He isn't going to fall to anything I can think of right now," Satan thought. "I guess I'll just leave Him alone for awhile…but I'll be back. That's one thing you can be sure of…I'll be back!"

APPLYING THE STORY

Satan tempted Jesus many times, and God tells us about three specific temptations in this story.

 Teacher's Note

Read the account of water from the rock in Exodus 17:1–7. Moses named the place Massah, which means temptation.

 Teaching Tip

As you share the account of water from the rock, trudge back and forth across the front of the classroom, with your head hanging low and a scowl on your face. Allow the children to see what complaining against and tempting the Lord looks like.

 Teaching Tip

You may wish to share Matthew 4:11b with your students: "behold, angels came and ministered unto him." Just as God had promised in Psalm 91, He cared for Jesus and sent His angels to provide for His every need.

What was the first temptation Satan brought to Jesus? (To make a stone into bread when Jesus was extremely hungry.) What did Jesus say to the devil when He was tempted? ("It is written…") Jesus used God's Word to defeat the temptation of the devil.

What was the second temptation the devil brought to Jesus? (To give Him all the kingdoms of the world if He would worship him.) What did Jesus say to the devil when He was tempted? ("It is written…") Again, Jesus used God's Word to defeat the temptation of the devil.

The third temptation was for Jesus to cast Himself down from the very highest part of the temple to prove that God the Father would send angels to keep Him safe. And, in this third temptation, Jesus again quoted Scripture to defeat the temptation of the devil.

Just think, Jesus, the Son of God, the Saviour of the world was tempted by Satan. If Jesus Himself was tempted, we can be sure that we will be tempted as well. But, while none of us look forward to being tempted, the wonderful and amazing part of all of this is that Jesus didn't use any special "magical" powers to defeat the temptations the devil brought His way. Jesus didn't do anything that you can't do.

Jesus was able to resist the devil's temptations because He was following the Holy Spirit, going where God wanted Him to go, and doing what God wanted Him to do. You can follow the Holy Spirit. He tells us in the Bible exactly how He wants us to live, and we can follow Him by obeying His Word. The Holy Spirit also speaks to us in our hearts, warning us when we are tempted to sin. You can listen to the Holy Spirit as He speaks to you, and you will have strength to resist temptation.

Jesus didn't only listen to the Holy Spirit in order to resist temptation—He also used Scripture against the lies of the devil.

When Jesus was a child, He read and memorized Scripture. You can do that. You can learn Bible verses that will help you resist the devil's temptations.

You will be tempted to disobey. You should learn Bible verses that you can use at times you are tempted to disobey:

Ephesians 6:1–3

1   *Children, obey your parents in the Lord: for this is right.*

2   *Honour thy father and mother; which is the first commandment with promise;*

3   *That it may be well with thee, and thou mayest live long on the earth.*

You will be tempted to lie. You should learn Bible verses you can use at times when you are tempted to lie:

Proverbs 12:22

22 Lying lips are abomination to the Lord: but they that deal truly are his delight.

Ephesians 4:25a

25a Wherefore putting away lying, speak every man truth with his neighbour:

You will be tempted to be unkind. You should learn Bible verses you can use to defeat the devil's temptation to be unkind:

Ephesians 4:32

32 And be ye kind one to another, tenderhearted, forgiving one another, even as God for Christ's sake hath forgiven you.

1 Corinthians 13:4a

4a Charity [love] suffereth long, and is kind;

You will be tempted to complain. You should learn Bible verses that will help you resist the devil's temptation to complain:

Numbers 11:1a

1a And when the people complained, it displeased the Lord:

You will be tempted to steal—to take something that doesn't belong to you. You should learn Bible verses that will help you resist the temptation to steal:

Exodus 20:15

15 Thou shalt not steal.

Ephesians 4:28

28 Let him that stole steal no more: but rather let him labour, working with his hands the thing which is good, that he may have to give to him that needeth.

Teaching Tip

Write the references on your chalkboard or dry erase board and quote or read the verse as you share the verses to overcome each temptation.

Example: Think, when you are tempted to lie, if you have these verses memorized, you can say "Proverbs 12:22—*Lying lips are abomination to the Lord: but they that deal truly are his delight.*"

I am choosing to deal truly, so I can be a delight to God.

As you grow older, you might be tempted to drink alcohol or to take drugs. You would be wise to learn Bible verses that will help you resist this temptation when the devil brings it your way:

Proverbs 20:1

1   Wine is a mocker, strong drink is raging: and whosoever is deceived thereby is not wise.

You will face these, and many more temptations, all throughout your life. The Bible teaches us that the devil is tricky, and he doesn't quit trying to tempt us to sin against God.

Satan makes his lies look good, and he tempts us to believe the good plans God has for us are boring, or that they won't make us popular or give us the kind of lives we really would like to have. The Bible tells us that Satan is a liar and a deceiver, and when we listen to him, we are tricked into believing things that really are not true.

The fun things that come into our lives through believing Satan and falling to his temptations only last a little while. They are tricks, the fun lasts only for a little while, and in the end, our lives will be unhappy.

Hebrews 11:25

25   Choosing rather to suffer affliction with the people of God, than to enjoy the pleasures of sin for a season.

God's Word is always true, and when you read it, believe it, memorize it, and use it against the devil's temptations, you will be doing exactly what Jesus did to overcome temptation. You will also be doing what millions of other Christians have done throughout the years as they followed Jesus and resisted temptations.

1 Corinthians 10:13

13   There hath no temptation taken you but such as is common to man: but God is faithful, who will not suffer you to be tempted above that ye are able; but will with the temptation also make a way to escape, that ye may be able to bear it.

- Other people have faced the temptation you are facing.
- God is faithful—we can trust Him to meet our needs and give us strength.
- God won't allow us to have temptations that are stronger than we are; with the help of the Holy Spirit and God's Word, we can resist.
- There is always a way to escape temptation.

We will not always be successful as we try to resist the devil. Sometimes we will fail—sometimes we will sin. When we sin, we must remember that God will always forgive us when we go to Him, telling Him that we know we have done wrong.

1 John 1:9

9   *If we confess our sins, he is faithful and just to forgive us our sins, and to cleanse us from all unrighteousness.*

God gives us all we need to resist temptation, and He gives us all we need to pick us back up when we fall. He is very good!

Review Game/Questions

Beware of the Roaring Lion!

Materials Needed

Visual for Roaring Lion game—found on the Ministry Resource CD.

Set up

Print both sides of the Roaring Lion game from the Ministry Resource CD. Cut out the squares. Before class set up a pocket chart or place cards in a bag.

Playing the Game

Divide class into teams. Ask review questions, alternating teams. When a student answers the question correctly, he may come to the front and pick one of the squares (either from the board or from the bag). The team receives the points from the back of the card, unless a roaring lion is picked, in which case no points are given for that turn. The winning team is the team with the most points.

1. Where did the Holy Spirit lead Jesus?

   Answer: To the wilderness

2. What was the wilderness like?

   Answer: It had mostly scrubby bushes and stones. Wild animals also lived there.

3. Why was Jesus led to the wilderness?

   Answer: To be tempted of the devil

4. How long did Jesus pray and fast in the wilderness?

   Answer: Forty days and forty nights

5. What was the first way the devil tempted Jesus?

   Answer: He tempted Him to turn the stones into bread, since Jesus was very hungry.

6. What was the second way the devil tempted Jesus?

   Answer: He offered to give Him all the kingdoms of the world if He would worship him.

7. What was the third way the devil tempted Jesus?
   Answer: He told Jesus to throw Himself off the temple to prove that God would send angels to keep Him safe.

8. How did Jesus respond to each temptation?
   Answer: He answered the devil's temptations with Scripture.

9. When the devil left Jesus, was it forever or was it only for a time?
   Answer: He left Him just for a time.

10. What is the best way to resist and fight against the lies and temptations of the devil?
    Answer: Read and memorize Scripture.

 # Teaching the Memory Verse

James 4:7

7 *Submit yourselves therefore to God. Resist the devil, and he will flee from you.*

Print memory verse visual from the Ministry Resource CD.

Did you know that no matter how strong you are, you are not strong enough to fight off the devil? We need super power, and that comes from God alone! God says to submit to Him, and He will give us the power to defeat the devil. "Submit" means to yield or to give over. God wants us to give over our lives to Him. The word "resist" means to succeed in ignoring the attraction of sin. So when we give our lives over to God, He will give us His power to ignore the attraction of what the devil has to offer.

Object Lesson—Tempted

Materials Needed:
Bowl full of candy (enough for every child to receive two pieces)

Lesson:
Hand one piece of candy to the children at the beginning of lesson time. Explain to the children that they can eat the piece of candy after the lesson but not during the lesson. Let them know they will be tempted to eat it during the lesson.

After the lesson is over have the children who did not eat the candy stand up. Once they are standing, have them choose another piece of candy out of the dish.

Application:
Ask the children how many of them were tempted to eat the candy during the lesson? Explain to the children that there is no temptation that is too great for them to overcome through the help of the Lord Jesus (1 Corinthians 10:13). Explain to them that the reason that they received another piece of candy is because God always blesses faithfulness.

 # Additional Resources

Find the following items on the Ministry Resource CD:
- Coloring Page (for younger children)
- Activity Page (for older children)
- Student Take-Home Paper
- PowerPoint Presentation

Craft—Puppet

Getting It Together

Small paper bag
Felt
Glue
Wiggle eyes
Pen

Per Student:

1   Verse template located on the Ministry Resource CD for each student
1   Paper bag
1   Piece of felt
1   Pair of wiggle eyes

Putting It Together

1.   Give each child a small paper bag, felt, glue & wiggle eyes.
2.   Take a piece of felt to make a hat and clothes.
3.   Cut out preprinted verse and glue onto the puppet.

Seeing It Together

Jesus has given us His Word to help us each day to turn from wrong and do right. When Jesus was in the wilderness the devil tempted Him. Jesus responded with the Word of God. As you make the puppet, remind each student to memorize God's Word just like Jesus did.

Suggested Classroom Schedule

Before Class		Complete attendance record. Provide students with coloring pages/activity pages.
Opening		Welcome
Prayer		Prayer requests and praise reports from the children
Song Time		
Memory Verse		John 12:26
Song Time		
Object Lesson		Following Jesus!
Bible Lesson		Jesus Calls His Disciples
Application/Invitation		Help saved students apply lesson. Invite unsaved students to receive Christ.
Snack		Bugle Snack Mix
Review Game/ Questions		Snowflakes
Craft		Spoon Fisherman
Closing		Give announcements and pray. Distribute take-home papers.

Lesson Eight Overview

Jesus Calls His Disciples

Theme— Jesus invites us to follow and serve Him.

Scripture
Matthew 4:18–23

Memory Verse
John 12:26—*"If any man serve me, let him follow me; and where I am, there shall also my servant be: if any man serve me, him will my Father honour."*

Lesson Outline

Introducing the Story
Today we will learn about the twelve men Jesus chose to be His disciples. Let's learn what qualities a person needs to be chosen by Jesus.

Telling the Story

1. **Jesus Sees Peter and Andrew** *(v. 18, John 1:40–42)* —*Flash Card 8.1*

2. **Jesus Calls Peter and Andrew to Follow Him** *(v. 19, 1 John 4:19)*

3. **Peter and Andrew Follow Jesus** *(v. 20)*

4. **Jesus Calls James and John** *(v. 21)*

5. **James and John Follow Jesus** *(v. 22, Luke 14:26)*

6. **Jesus Teaches and Preaches** *(v. 23)*

7. **Jesus Calls Other Disciples** *(Mark 3:14)*—*Flash Card 8.2*

Applying the Story *(Ephesians 6:1, John 16:33)*—*Flash Card 8.3*
Anyone who has trusted Jesus as his Saviour can be Jesus' disciple. In fact, Jesus wants everyone who has trusted in Him to be His disciple. You can be a good disciple by spending time with Jesus and telling others about Him. Who can you tell this week about what Jesus has done for you and what He did on the cross?

8 Lesson Eight

Jesus Calls His Disciples

Theme: Jesus invites us to follow and serve Him.

 ## Scripture

Matthew 4:18–23

18 And Jesus, walking by the sea of Galilee, saw two brethren, Simon called Peter, and Andrew his brother, casting a net into the sea: for they were fishers.

19 And he saith unto them, Follow me, and I will make you fishers of men.

20 And they straightway left their nets, and followed him.

21 And going on from thence, he saw other two brethren, James the son of Zebedee, and John his brother, in a ship with Zebedee their father, mending their nets; and he called them.

22 And they immediately left the ship and their father, and followed him.

23 And Jesus went about all Galilee, teaching in their synagogues, and preaching the gospel of the kingdom, and healing all manner of sickness and all manner of disease among the people.

Memory Verse

John 12:26

"If any man serve me, let him follow me; and where I am, there shall also my servant be: if any man serve me, him will my Father honour."

Teacher's Checklist

Bugle Snack Mix
You will need bugles, pretzels, chocolate chips, and mini marshmallows. As the students munch on their bugle snack mix, remind them to listen to Jesus as He speaks to and directs us day by day.

- ❏ Read Matthew 4:18–23 daily.

- ❏ Study Lesson Eight.

- ❏ Flash cards 8.1–8.3

- ❏ Prepare snack—Bugle Snack Mix.

- ❏ Print and cut out "Snowflakes" review game from Ministry Resource CD.

- ❏ Print this week's memory verse (James 12:26) from the Ministry Resource CD.

- ❏ Print memory verse paper strips from the Ministry Resource CD.

- ❏ Gather for object lesson—Bible and yarn.

- ❏ Purchase for craft—wiggle craft eyes (2 per student).

- ❏ Print for craft—verse template from the Ministry Resource CD.

- ❏ Gather for craft—plastic spoons, ribbon, glue, yarn, material, and paper.

- ❏ Print and duplicate Coloring Pages or Activity Pages on the Ministry Resource CD (one per student).

- ❏ Print and duplicate Take-Home Paper on the Ministry Resource CD (one per student).

 **Bible Lesson**

Scripture: Matthew 4:18–23

INTRODUCING THE STORY

Have you ever been in a group—at school or on some other activity—where you were going to play a game, and everyone had to be divided up into teams? Maybe the teacher or leader chose two students to be the team captains, and then the captains took turns choosing team members.

"Shawn," calls out the first captain, and Shawn smiles as he runs over to be on Team 1.

"Garrett," calls out the second captain, and Garrett, glad he was chosen right away, hops up and jumps over to be on Team 2.

Back and forth, the captains take turns picking members for their teams.

The two captains are feeling excited, and Shawn and Garrett are feeling excited, because they know they don't have to worry about being chosen last. The other kids who are chosen near the beginning are happy, too. But you, maybe, or some other students, aren't feeling so excited. Almost all the students have been chosen, and you are still waiting.

Have you ever noticed that some people are always chosen last? Maybe they aren't very good at the sport that is being played, or maybe they aren't very popular, or maybe there is something about them that makes them different from most people—whatever the reason, they are always chosen at the end.

And, sadly, that's often the way it is in the world. The biggest and strongest get picked first. The little guy who's not very fast ends up on the team of whoever had to choose last. Then, he's the last one to bat, the last one to serve, or the last one on the bench, waiting to play.

Jesus did some choosing when He was on earth. Listen as we find out what qualities a person needed to be chosen by Jesus.

 **Teaching Tip**

Choose names to fit your class—gender, age, etc.

Make this personal by acting as both team captains, calling students to each team. Be sure to call the least-likely-to-be-chosen near the beginning!

THE STORY

1. Jesus Sees Peter and Andrew (v. 18)

Flash Card 8.1

"Why do you suppose we got to be the lucky ones—being able to meet the Messiah?" Peter asked his brother Andrew. "I sure thank you for introducing me to Him after you met Him. I remember how excited you were, and I can still hear you, 'We have found the Messiah!' Every time I think of you looking for me as soon as you met Jesus, so I could meet Him too, I feel thankful all over again."

"I know what you mean," answered Andrew. "We have heard about the Messiah all our lives—God promised to send Him hundreds of years ago—and now He's here, and we actually got to meet Him!"

John 1:40–42

40   One of the two which heard John speak, and followed him, was Andrew, Simon Peter's brother.

41   He first findeth his own brother Simon, and saith unto him, We have found the Messias, which is, being interpreted, the Christ.

42   And he brought him to Jesus. And when Jesus beheld him, he said, Thou art Simon the son of Jona: thou shalt be called Cephas, which is by interpretation, A stone.

"Think of it," said Peter. "We're just a couple of smelly old fishermen. We haven't gone to college, we aren't rich, we don't have fancy clothes, we're not religious leaders—and we smell like fish! But, for some reason, God chose us to meet the Messiah…I wonder why."

Peter and Andrew continued their work in silence. They each grabbed a side of the heavy fishing net, lifted it, and lowered it back into the water. "Great day for fishing," said Peter, as he wiped the water off his forehead with the end of his sleeve.

"Yep," said Andrew, "It looks like it's going to be a good day."

Both brothers looked up at the same time, to see a man walking along the beach. "Who do you suppose it is?" they each wondered, as they lifted their hands over their eyes to shield them from the bright sun in order to get a better look.

"Hey, it's Jesus," Peter almost shouted. "It's Him—the Messiah! I'd know Him anywhere!"

"Look!" Andrew hollered back. "He's coming toward us!"

Jesus had already seen the brothers, long before they noticed Him. He smiled as He came to where they were fishing—the kind of smile that made them know He really cared about them and wanted to be with them.

2. Jesus Calls Peter and Andrew to Follow Him (v. 19)

As Jesus came near Andrew and Peter, He thought about the first time they had met. He remembered Andrew's cheerful personality and how glad He had felt when Andrew was so happy to meet Him. He thought about how pleased He was when Andrew ran off right away to find his brother, Peter, to bring Him to Jesus.

He remembered Peter, too. Peter was strong, and he loved to talk. He thought about how Peter had looked at Him with such admiration. He knew both these men were full of desire to serve Him.

There they were, on the Sea of Galilee—Andrew and Peter wondering as they watched Jesus coming toward them, and Jesus looking at them like He had known them all their lives. He had the kindest face they had ever seen. As Jesus smiled at them, they knew He—the Messiah—loved them and wanted to be with them. And they wanted to be with Him, too.

1 John 4:19

19   We love him, because he first loved us.

Then, Jesus looked at Andrew and Peter with the kind of look that captures your attention. Peter saw Jesus' mouth begin to move, as if He was about to say something. Andrew noticed the same thing, and at the same time, the two brothers looked at each other out of the corners of their eyes, as if to say, "Get ready—Jesus is going to say something!"

Then they heard the words of Christ—the most wonderful words they could ever imagine hearing. Jesus actually said to them—to these two smelly fishermen whom most of the townspeople avoided, because they smelled so bad—"Follow me, and I will make you fishers of men."

3. Peter and Andrew Follow Jesus (v. 20)

"Fishers of men—us? Think of it, fishers of smelly fish, fishing for men! Jesus wants us to follow Him, and He will make us into men who fish for men instead of fishing for fish—men who spend their lives telling people the good news that the Messiah is here. Jesus actually wants us!

"And you know what? We can learn to do it! We know how to fish—Jesus isn't asking us to do something we could never learn how to do. He's just calling us to do what we're already doing—it's just men instead of fish!

"And they straightway left their nets, and followed him." Andrew and Peter didn't even need to think about their decision. Jesus, the Messiah, wanted them! And they wanted Him. Yes, they would follow Him immediately. And so they did.

4. Jesus Calls James and John (v. 21)

Teacher's Note

Disciple: a learner; a follower; an adherent to the doctrines of another. Hence the constant attendants of Christ were called His disciples; and hence all Christians are called His disciples, as they profess to learn and receive His doctrines and precepts.

Jesus continued His walk along the Sea of Galilee, but He was no longer alone. Andrew and his brother, Peter, now walked beside Him. The two brothers kept looking at each other in disbelief. "I can't believe this is really happening to us," each one thought. "The Messiah has come, and He has chosen us to be His followers—His disciples."

As they walked along the beach of the Sea of Galilee, Jesus pointed to the boat of their friends, James and John. "Friends of yours, aren't they?" Jesus asked Andrew and Peter.

"Oh, yes," replied Peter. "We've known them all our lives. Their father, Zebedee, is one of the best fishermen on the sea—everyone wants to work for him. He has taught his sons to fish as well as he does, and they all work together, along with many others. That's their dad's boat they are in right now."

When fishermen use their nets all the time, as Zebedee and his sons did, the nets often rip, and they need to be repaired. That's what James and John were doing that very day—sitting in the boat, sewing up the torn net.

"I wonder if we'll be doing this all our lives—fishing I mean," said James to his brother.

"I guess so," answered John. "We have got the best boat on the sea, and we've been taught by the most skilled fisherman. I love my life as a fisherman. Why, I guess the only thing I love more than our father, our family, the sea, and my job is God."

"That's just how I feel," James said, as he tied another piece of rope around the torn net.

They both heard their names, and they looked up. "Follow me," Jesus was calling them from the beach.

5. James and John Follow Jesus (v. 22)

James and John recognized Jesus immediately. "It's the Messiah!" They knew then and there that they wanted to follow the Messiah more than they wanted anything else in the whole world. They loved their father, they loved their family, they loved the sea, and they loved their job; but they loved God more. And there, right beside their boat, was the Messiah, the Son of God, inviting them to follow Him.

"Why us?" they wondered. "We're nobody special. We haven't had any special training. We've studied the Bible with our father, but we aren't religious leaders or anything. We aren't rich or famous. We're just poor, smelly fishermen—why would Jesus want us?"

James and John looked at their friends, Andrew and Peter, standing beside Jesus. Andrew and Peter had never looked so peaceful and happy.

"And they immediately left the ship, and their father, and followed him."

Luke 14:26

26   *If any man come to me, and hate not his father, and mother, and wife, and children, and brethren, and sisters, yea, and his own life also, he cannot be my disciple.*

Teaching Tip

You may wish to share that they didn't leave their father alone, with no one to care for him. "And they left their father Zebedee in the ship with the hired servants, and went after him" (Mark 1:20b).

"Hate" in Luke 14:26 is a comparison. It means to love less. It simply means we are to love Jesus far above anyone or anything else, making Him first in our lives.

The disciples loved Jesus best, and they sacrificed all to follow Him.

6. Jesus Teaches and Preaches (v. 23)

"We haven't really given up anything, have we?" Andrew said to Peter, as they listened to Jesus preach.

"No," answered Peter. "We've learned more about God in the short time since we've been following the Messiah than we ever knew."

"He's taught us how to preach, and He's taught us how to teach," continued John. "Imagine, the Messiah is our Teacher!"

"I'm sure glad our fathers taught us how to work," laughed James. "Because it sure is a busy life we are living. I'm so glad to be able to serve Jesus."

John said, "We've seen Him perform so many miracles. Remember when He gave sight to the blind man, and when He healed the woman who couldn't walk?"

And so, Peter and Andrew, James and John followed Jesus, going where He went, doing what He did, and learning what He taught them. They were so glad to be His disciples.

7. Jesus Calls Other Disciples (Mark 3:14)

Flash Card 8.2

Jesus called other men to be His followers—His disciples—as well. In all, Jesus called twelve men to be His special followers, who would go where

He went and do what He did. As He taught them to preach, He knew one day they would each go off on their own, telling others about Jesus, the Saviour of the world.

Flash Card 8.3

APPLYING THE STORY

Jesus chose all different kinds of men to be His twelve disciples. Some of them, like Peter, James, and John were well known; and we read of them all throughout the New Testament. For others of them, we only know that Jesus chose them to be His disciples and that they followed Him.

One of the disciples was named Matthew (also called Levi). He was a tax collector, and tax collectors were known for being dishonest and taking more money from the people than the people owed. No one liked tax collectors. Who would have ever thought Jesus would call a tax collector to follow Him?

But Matthew was a dishonest tax collector before he trusted Jesus; and when he trusted Jesus, his whole life changed, just like Jesus knew it would.

After Matthew trusted Jesus and followed Him, just as Andrew, Peter, James and John had done, he invited his tax collector friends to a big meal at his house. He invited Jesus and the other disciples, too, and Jesus told all those rich, dishonest tax collectors that they should trust Him as their Saviour, too.

Jesus chooses all kinds of people to follow Him:

- Rich
- Poor
- Strong
- Weak
- Educated
- Uneducated
- Popular
- Unpopular
- Handsome or pretty
- Ordinary looking
- People who have been taught the Bible all their lives
- People who are from families who haven't taught them the Bible

In fact, Jesus chooses everyone to be His disciples. You don't have to be the smartest, the biggest, the fastest runner, the richest, or the prettiest. You don't have to come from a rich family, and your dad doesn't have to be a preacher in order for Jesus to choose you as His disciple.

And God doesn't choose only poor, smelly fishermen or dishonest tax collectors to be His disciples.

God has only one requirement for someone to be His disciple. We have to want to be His disciple—we have to want to follow Him. He calls to us "Follow me, and I will make you fishers of men," just as He invited Andrew and Peter; but He doesn't make us or force us to follow Him. He chooses to make us His disciple, but we have to make the choice to follow Him.

Anyone who has trusted Jesus as his or her Saviour can be Jesus' disciple. In fact, Jesus wants everyone who has trusted in Him to be His disciple. But, no one can be Jesus' disciple until he or she has first trusted Jesus as his or her Saviour.

Maybe you have been trying to be a disciple without first being saved. When you trust Jesus as your Saviour, He helps you be His disciple. He gives you strength and courage to follow Him. It's so hard to try to follow Jesus when He isn't your Saviour. Just as we said last week that you cannot earn your salvation by being baptized, you can not earn your salvation by trying to follow Jesus. You need to choose to trust Jesus first.

Have you ever been saved? If you don't remember for sure or if in your heart right now you have a question about it, please talk to me after class. I would like to explain more about it to you and help you trust Jesus.

Now, how do you answer Jesus' invitation to be His disciple? Do you remember what Peter and Andrew did when Jesus called them to be fishers of men? (They left their nets and followed Him.) Do you remember what James and John did when Jesus called them to follow Him? (They immediately left the ship and their father and followed Him.)

Now, it isn't time for you to leave your parents—children don't have to leave their parents in order to follow Jesus. In fact, in order for children to really follow Jesus, they need to obey their parents. That is what Jesus calls children who are His followers to do.

Ephesians 6:1

1   Children, obey your parents in the Lord: for this is right.

But, like Peter, Andrew, James, John, and the other disciples, you do need to leave something in order to follow Jesus. You need to leave your way, and choose God's way. You need to decide—as the twelve disciples did—to want what Jesus wants, like what Jesus likes, go where Jesus would go, and do what Jesus would do.

The disciples learned to think like Jesus thought by listening to what He had to say. Since the Bible is the Word of God, you can listen to Jesus speak by reading

Act It Out

Follow the Leader
End this lesson with a "Follow the Leader" activity. Have your students follow you around the room, duplicating your actions, as you pull out a chair and push it back in, pat the top of your head, clap your hands, etc. Reward them somewhere during the activity with a small piece of candy or other treat, such as gummy fish or goldfish crackers, reminding them that there is great reward in following Christ.

the Bible. Every morning when you wake up, remind yourself that you want to be Jesus' disciple and that you will have to leave your way of playing, watching TV, or whatever else you usually do first thing in the morning so you can read God's Word first. Then ask Him to help you do what He taught you in the Bible that very day.

The disciples learned to like what Jesus liked and want what He wanted by watching Him, and making the choices He made. They watched how He treated people. They noticed what He chose to do with His time. They saw that Jesus spoke kindly, so they left their own ways of speaking and spoke kindly like Jesus. They noticed He spent His time telling people about salvation, so they told people how to be saved. You can treat people the way Jesus treated them and spend your time doing things Jesus would do. You can serve others as Jesus did. You can be patient with others as Jesus was. You can tell others what Jesus has done for you and what He did for them on the cross. You can submit to authority as Jesus did. You can be His disciple!

And when you make the decision to be a disciple of Jesus, He will give you peace and happiness deep down in your heart that you will never have when you live for yourself instead of for the Lord.

John 16:33

33   *These things I have spoken unto you, that in me ye might have peace. In the world ye shall have tribulation: but be of good cheer; I have overcome the world.*

Review Game/Questions

Snowflakes

Materials Needed
Visuals for Snowflakes game found on the Ministry Resource CD.

Set up
Print both sides of the Snowflakes game on cardstock. Cut out squares. Laminate for durability. Display the Snowflakes game pieces in front of the students. You may add velcro or a magnetic strip on the back of each game piece. You can also place game pieces in a bag.

Playing the Game

Each row is a team. Begin asking review questions. When a student answers a question correctly, have that student come forward and pick a snowflake and follow the instructions on the back of the snowflake (for his team). The row with the highest points wins the game.

1. Who were the first two fishermen mentioned in our story?
    Answer: Peter and Andrew

2. What was the occupation of Peter and Andrew?
    Answer: They were fishermen.

3. When Jesus called Andrew and Peter to follow Him, He told them they would fish for something other than fish. What was it?
    Answer: They would be fishers of men.

4. How did Andrew and Peter respond to Jesus' call to be fishers of men?
    Answer: They left their nets and followed Him immediately.

5. What were James and John doing when Jesus called them to follow Him?
    Answer: They were repairing their fishing nets.

6. How did James and John respond to Jesus' call to follow Him?
    Answer: They left their ship and followed Him immediately.

7. Name some things these brothers were able to witness Jesus doing.
    Answer: They saw Jesus teach, preach, and perform miracles.

8. Jesus called other men to be disciples, too. How many did He call?
    Answer: He called twelve men to be His special followers.

9. Were all of Jesus' disciples fishermen? What occupation did Matthew have?
    Answer: No! He was a tax collector.

10. Jesus has called you to be His disciple, too. In what ways can you follow Him right now?
    Answer: We can follow Him by leaving bad things, by reading our Bibles, and by striving to be like Him.

Teaching the Memory Verse

John 12:26

26   If any man serve me, let him follow me; and where I am, there shall also my servant be: if any man serve me, him will my Father honour.

Jesus invites anyone to serve Him. What a privilege to be able to serve the king of kings. When we serve the Lord and follow Him, God promises to honor us!

Introduce one flash card at a time, repeating each phrase a few times before adding the next flash card. When the students have a grasp of the verse, play the game "Telephone."

Telephone
Materials needed
Print and cut the word strips for John 12:26. (Twice)

Playing the Game
Divide the class evenly into two teams. Have each team arrange themselves in a straight line or circle. Give one member of each team the same strip. When you say go, they whisper in the ear of the student next to them. Then that person whispers in the ear of the person next to them. This continues until the statement reaches the last person on the team. That person runs and whispers in the ear of the teacher what was on the strip. If the student repeats the statement word for word, that team scores a point.

Object Lesson—Following Jesus!

Materials Needed:
Bible
Yarn

Lesson:
Unroll the yarn and lay it on the floor like a path. Call all of the children over to follow you along this path. While you are walking, carry the Bible high above you, allowing the children to follow you and the Word of God. As you and the children are walking along the path lead them in motions like touching their nose, clapping hands, or hopping on one foot.

Application:
Explain to the children that God wants us to follow His Word all the days of our lives (Proverbs 3:6).

Craft—Spoon Fisherman

Getting It Together
Plastic spoons
Ribbon
Glue
Yarn
Material
Paper

Per student:
2 Wiggly craft eyes
1 Verse template on Ministry Resource CD

Putting It Together
1. Cut a small piece of ribbon.
2. Glue in place on the spoon.
3. Glue yarn for hair and a small piece of material on the head.
4. Tie ribbon around the hat.
5. Cut a fish out of paper and glue it on.
6. Print out the memory verse.
7. Roll into a scroll and glue on the puppet.

Seeing It Together
Just like Jesus called His disciples, He is calling for each boy and girl to follow Him. When each student makes and plays with the fisherman puppet, remind each student to follow and tell other people about Jesus.

 # Additional Resources

Find the following items on the Ministry Resource CD:
- Coloring Page (for younger children)
- Activity Page (for older children)
- Student Take-Home Paper
- PowerPoint Presentation

Suggested Classroom Schedule

Before Class	Complete attendance record. Provide students with coloring pages/activity pages.
Opening	Welcome
Prayer	Prayer requests and praise reports from the children
Song Time	
Memory Verse	John 3:7
Song Time	
Object Lesson	Invisible Wind
Bible Lesson	Jesus Meets Nicodemus
Application/Invitation	Help saved students apply lesson. Invite unsaved students to receive Christ.
Snack	Baby in a Blanket
Review Game/ Questions	Candy Jeopardy
Craft	"God So Loved" Ruler
Closing	Give announcements and pray. Distribute take-home papers.

Lesson Nine Overview

Jesus Meets Nicodemus

Theme—You must be born again to see Heaven.

Scripture
John 3:1–16

Memory Verse
John 3:7 — *"Marvel not that I said unto thee, Ye must be born again."*

Lesson Outline

Introducing the Story
In the story today, we will learn about a man that Jesus spoke to. Jesus helped this man understand what it means to be born again.

Telling the Story
1. Nicodemus, a Ruler of the Jews (v. 1)—*Flash Card 9.1*
2. Nicodemus Goes to Jesus at Night (v. 2)—*Flash Card 9.2*
3. Jesus Answers Nicodemus (v. 3, Ephesians 2:8–9)
4. Nicodemus Doesn't Understand (v. 4)
5. Ye Must Be Born Again (vv. 5–8, Romans 5:12, James 2:10)
6. Nicodemus Still Doesn't Understand (v. 9)
7. Jesus Explains (vv. 10–15)—*Flash Card 9.3*
8. Jesus Explains God's Gifts of Eternal Life (v. 16, *John 14:6*)

Applying the Story
The only way we can go to Heaven is by being born again—by believing in Jesus to save us from our sin.

9 Lesson Nine

Jesus Meets Nicodemus

Theme: You must be born again to see Heaven.

Scripture

John 3:1–16

1   There was a man of the Pharisees, named Nicodemus, a ruler of the Jews:

2   The same came to Jesus by night, and said unto him, Rabbi, we know that thou art a teacher come from God: for no man can do these miracles that thou doest, except God be with him.

3   Jesus answered and said unto him, Verily, verily, I say unto thee, Except a man be born again, he cannot see the kingdom of God.

4   Nicodemus saith unto him, How can a man be born when he is old? can he enter the second time into his mother's womb, and be born?

5   Jesus answered, Verily, verily, I say unto thee, Except a man be born of water and of the Spirit, he cannot enter into the kingdom of God.

6   That which is born of the flesh is flesh; and that which is born of the Spirit is spirit.

7   Marvel not that I said unto thee, Ye must be born again.

8   The wind bloweth where it listeth, and thou hearest the sound thereof, but canst not tell whence it cometh, and whither it goeth: so is every one that is born of the Spirit.

9   Nicodemus answered and said unto him, How can these things be?

10   Jesus answered and said unto him, Art thou a master of Israel, and knowest not these things?

11   Verily, verily, I say unto thee, We speak that we do know, and testify that we have seen; and ye receive not our witness.

12   If I have told you earthly things, and ye believe not, how shall ye believe, if I tell you of heavenly things?

13   And no man hath ascended up to heaven, but he that came down from heaven, even the Son of man which is in heaven.

14   And as Moses lifted up the serpent in the wilderness, even so must the Son of man be lifted up:

15 *That whosoever believeth in him should not perish, but have eternal life.*

16 *For God so loved the world, that he gave his only begotten Son, that whosoever believeth in him should not perish, but have everlasting life.*

Teacher's Checklist

❑ Read John 3:1–16 daily.

❑ Study Lesson Nine.

❑ Flash cards 9.1–9.2

❑ Prepare snack—Marshmallows and Fruit Roll Ups.

❑ Print "Candy Jeopardy" question cards from Ministry Resource CD.

❑ Purchase candy for review game.

❑ Purchase for object lesson—one balloon per student.

❑ Print for craft—ruler and globe from the Ministry Resource CD.

❑ Gather for craft—paper, glue, and crayons.

❑ Print and duplicate Coloring Pages or Activity Pages on the Ministry Resource CD (one per student).

❑ Print and duplicate Take-Home Paper on the Ministry Resource CD (one per student).

Baby in a Blanket
Take a large marshmallow and fruit roll up. Fold the fruit roll up corner to corner to make a triangle. With the triangle pointed down, place the marshmallow on the top, half on the fruit roll up and half off. Fold the right corner over the marshmallow. Fold the left corner over the marshmallow. Fold the bottom corner making a diaper. Use candy or frosting to make a face.

 **Bible Lesson**

Scripture: John 3:1–16

INTRODUCING THE STORY

Have you ever been in a tornado or a hurricane? Or have you ever seen pictures on the news of the damage done by a tornado or hurricane?

Tornados and hurricanes are storms in which there are great, strong winds. The wind blows so hard and so strong that it sometimes destroys buildings, cars, and trees. We can easily see the damage done by these strong winds.

Then, there are other winds—gentle winds. We are glad to feel them on a hot summer day. They dry the perspiration off our faces and gently blow our hair. We can see the leaves on the tree blow from the wind. These are pleasant winds.

There are winds with rain and winds with snow. There are warm winds, hot winds, cool winds, and cold winds. And we can see the things that happen as a result of these winds. We see the sand blow and the grass rustle.

But, we can never actually see the wind itself—we only see what the wind does.

Wind is an amazing creation of God, and Jesus spoke about wind to teach a man in the Bible about how God works.

 Teaching Tip

Encourage students to share storm experiences. When they share life experiences with you in class, they connect more readily with what you are teaching. Also, you gain insight into their lives through their stories. By noticing the people they include in their accounts, and how your students perceived the actions of those people, you can discern details of the lives of your students that will help you relate to them.

THE STORY

1. Nicodemus, a Ruler of the Jews (v. 1)

Flash Card 9.1

Nicodemus watched and listened as Jesus spoke to a great crowd of people. As Nicodemus listened, he was thinking, "I have studied the Old Testament all of my life. I am one of the most religious people in all of Israel. In fact, I am one of the greatest religious leaders! I teach other people about the Word of God. I live according to the law. I always try to do the right thing. I am a Jew—one of God's special people. If anybody would be able to go to Heaven, it would be me. I'm so good.

"And yet, what Jesus is saying is different from anything I've ever heard or anything I've ever taught. And the miracles He is doing—not just anyone could do what He has done. I know that in order to do these miracles, He has

 **Teaching Tip**

Help your students understand how large this crowd would have been by providing examples of how many classrooms the size of yours would be filled by this great crowd.

to have been sent from God. If He is from God, then I should believe what He says, because God knows all things. But His teachings are opposite of everything I've ever believed—everything I've ever done.

"The other religious leaders reject Jesus' teaching. They are jealous of Jesus, and they say that what He says is not true. But, somehow, I believe Jesus speaks the truth. I believe He really is sent by God."

Flash Card 9.2   2. Nicodemus Goes to Jesus at Night (v. 2)

"I've got to talk to Jesus—I need to find out the truth," thought Nicodemus. "Now, how can I meet with Him alone? He's always surrounded by a crowd of people. What would the people think if they saw me asking Jesus questions? They know I am one of the most educated religious leaders in all of Israel, and they think I know everything there is to know about religious matters. I don't want everybody to know that I have questions—they come to me for answers to their questions. And, I really don't want the other Pharisees to see me talking to Him. They would think less of me if they saw me asking Jesus questions.

"Another thing, if I just go up and start talking to Jesus, we will be interrupted a hundred times. So many people have questions for Jesus, and if others talk to Him while I am trying to find out the truth, I won't learn everything I want to know.

"I know what I'll do. The crowds are around Jesus all day, but at night they go home to their families. When it is night, and everyone has gone home for supper, I will go to Jesus. I will find out the truth from Him—tonight!"

And that is what Nicodemus did. He waited for night to come. The day seemed so long to Nicodemus as he watched the endless crowds gathered around Jesus. All day long he heard Jesus preaching and teaching, and yet, He didn't understand what Jesus meant.

All day long, Nicodemus thought about what he would say to Jesus and what Jesus would say to him. "I'm a religious leader—I was taught by the finest teachers," Nicodemus told himself. "I'll tell Jesus that—so He can know exactly who He's talking to…No, somehow I think He already knows who I am. Somehow, I think that the things I've already learned and done won't really matter. I'll just tell Him who I think He is, and I'll hear what He has to say."

Finally, it began to get dark. Nicodemus grew excited, and a little nervous, as he smelled the meat being roasted and the bread being baked for the evening meals. He knew those smells meant that soon the crowds would go home, and Jesus would be free to talk privately with Nicodemus.

Nicodemus had kept his eye on Jesus all day, and he knew exactly where Jesus was. When the last person had gone home, Nicodemus quietly stepped up to Jesus, cleared his throat, and said, "(Ahem) We know You are a teacher that has come from God, and we admire You. We can tell You are from God because of the great miracles You have done. They prove that You are from God. No one could do these miracles unless God was with him."

3. Jesus Answers Nicodemus (v. 3)

Jesus looked deep into Nicodemus' eyes, and Nicodemus looked back into the most honest and loving eyes he had ever seen. Jesus' answer to Nicodemus was full of meaning. "I am glad you have been thinking, Nicodemus. You know all about religious things. You've studied religion all your life."

Jesus spoke to Nicodemus, "Listen to what I am going to say, Nicodemus—it is the truth; and it is different from everything you've ever heard, everything you've ever thought, and everything you've ever taught other people. I know you, just like all the other religious people, think you will go to Heaven because you are a Jew. And you and all the other religious people think being good will take you to Heaven. But the truth is, Nicodemus, it's not enough. Being a Jew, and being good, will never take you to Heaven. 'Except a man be born again, he cannot see the kingdom of God.' It's not the way you've always thought it was, Nicodemus."

Ephesians 2:8–9

8   *For by grace are ye saved through faith; and that not of yourselves: it is the gift of God:*

9   *Not of works, lest any man should boast.*

4. Nicodemus Doesn't Understand (v. 4)

"I'll just have to be honest with Jesus, and I'll tell Him I don't understand at all what He's talking about," Nicodemus said to himself. "I mean, I understand

Womb: the special place God made in a mother, where a baby lives and receives everything he or she needs (food, vitamins, etc.) until he/she is born

about a baby being born, but Jesus is talking about something I don't know anything about." Then, to Jesus, he said, "Are you telling me that a person has to go back into his mother's womb, where he was before he was born—can a person go back into his mother's womb and be born a second time?"

5. Ye Must Be Born Again (vv. 5–8)

"The truth is so different from what you are used to hearing, Nicodemus. You have lived your life thinking you knew best. You have thought your religious life and your religious rules would take you to Heaven. You haven't really tried to find out what is true. You haven't thought about spiritual things."

"This is what I mean," Jesus said. "In order for a person to be saved from his sin, and in order for a person to understand spiritual truth, he has to have a new birth. This is not the birth of the body I am talking about—it is the birth of the spirit."

Listen closely, so you can understand what Jesus was talking about when He said a person has to be born again to go to Heaven. You see, back in the Garden of Eden, when Adam and Eve sinned, their spirits—the part of them that could actually know God and have a relationship with God—died. Since that time, every person who has been born has sinned, just like Adam and Eve, and their spirits are dead also.

> **Romans 5:12**
>
> 12 *Wherefore, as by one man sin entered into the world, and death by sin; and so death passed upon all men, for that all have sinned:*

It is the spirit of a person that needs to be born again in order for him or her to go to Heaven and in order for him or her to understand spiritual things.

Your spirit needs to be born again by the Spirit of God through the Word of God. You see, Nicodemus had been thinking that it is the outside of a person that needs to be clean in order for you to go to Heaven. That is why he tried to be so careful to keep all the commandments and obey the law. And no matter how hard he tried, he still disobeyed the law. He still broke the commandments. Even if he had only broken one commandment, he would still be a sinner and would need to have his sins forgiven. Every person is a sinner, just like Adam.

James 2:10

10   *For whosoever shall keep the whole law, and yet offend in one point, he is guilty of all.*

It is the inside of a person that needs to be clean—the spirit. Nicodemus looked at the outside of a person, and thought that if he looked religious and good on the outside, he was a good person whom God will surely allow to go to Heaven. But God looks on the inside of a person. He knows whether or not that person's spirit has been born again by God's Holy Spirit inside of him.

Jesus could see that Nicodemus didn't really understand what He had said. "The wind blows," Jesus said to Nicodemus. "It blows wherever it wants to blow, and you can hear the sound of it. Now, you can't see the wind itself—you can only see what the wind has done. You can see the leaves blow from the wind. You can feel the wind on your face. You can hear the wind whistle through the trees. You can see the sand blow across the ground. But you can't see the wind. You can't really understand how the wind works—how it changes direction, how it blows sometimes strong and sometimes gentle—you just have to believe it's there.

"That's what the spiritual birth—being born again—is like. You can't see or understand the Holy Spirit and how He works to make a person born again. You just have to believe that it's true, and when you trust Him to give you the new birth, then you will be able to see what He does. You will notice Him changing you on the inside."

6. Nicodemus Still Doesn't Understand (v. 9)

"Nicodemus answered and said unto him, How can these things be?" He said, "Jesus, I'm just going to let You teach me the truth. You be the teacher, and I'll be the student. Tell me what You mean."

7. Jesus Explains (vv. 10–15)

Flash Card 9.3

Jesus knew He had to make Nicodemus understand, and He knew He would have to get Nicodemus to see for himself that his own way was the wrong way. Jesus looked at Nicodemus with the same honest and loving eyes Nicodemus had noticed when they first met, and Jesus asked him a question, "Nicodemus, are you one of the great religious teachers of Israel, and yet you don't know what

I'm talking about? You, who have studied and taught the Old Testament—you, of all people—should understand about the need to have your sins forgiven. This truth is taught all throughout the Old Testament.

"I know the truth, and I speak the truth, and you and the other religious leaders haven't accepted it. Now, when I talk to you about things you have experienced—things like babies being born and the wind—you don't accept it. How will you believe if I speak to you about spiritual things?

"Everything I tell you comes straight from the Father in Heaven. No man has gone to Heaven and come back; but I have come from Heaven, because I am God the Son. Believe Me, that what I say is the truth.

"You have read in the Old Testament about the time when Moses was leading the Jews to the land God promised to them. The people sinned against God, and they said God wasn't taking care of them; and God allowed the people to be bitten by snakes. There were thousands of snakes, and thousands of people were bitten. Many people even died.

"Everyone was so afraid. Some of the people went to Moses, and they said, 'We know we have sinned against God. Please tell Him we're sorry and ask Him to take these snakes away!'

"Moses talked to God, and God told him to make a snake out of brass—a very shiny metal that looks like gold. God told Moses to put the brass snake at the end of a very long pole and to walk past all the people, carrying the pole with the snake on it. If a person had been bitten by a snake, all the person had to do was to look at the brass snake, and he wouldn't die, but he would live!

"I know, it wasn't the way they thought they would be healed. They thought God would just heal them from their snake bites because they wanted to be healed. But that wasn't God's way. God's way was for them to trust Him—that's why He told them to look at the snake in order to be healed.

"It's the same with eternal life—being born again—Nicodemus. People think they can go to Heaven just because they want to go there. But that isn't God's way. Just as a person who had been bitten by a snake would live only if he looked at the brass snake, a person who is a sinner (and that is every person) needs to look to Me, Jesus, in order to live forever in Heaven. The only way for a snake-bitten person to live was to look up at the brass snake, and the only way for a sinner to live forever in Heaven is to look up to Me to save him or her.

"And whoever looks to Me, believing in Me to save him or her, will not have to go to the Lake of Fire, but will live with Me in Heaven forever."

Teaching Tip

You can read the account of this story in Numbers 21:5–9.

Use an Object

Brass Snake
Paint a toy snake with gold spray paint and attach it to the end of a broom handle or other long pole. As you speak of looking up at the serpent, lift the snake on the pole. Also lift it up when you speak of looking up to Jesus.

8. Jesus Explains God's Gift of Eternal Life (v. 16)

"For God so loved the world, that he gave his only begotten Son, that whosoever believeth in him should not perish, but have everlasting life." Jesus reminded Nicodemus, "It's not like you thought, Nicodemus. It's not being good, going to church, or being a Jew that will take you to Heaven when you die. Nobody can be good enough to go to Heaven—all people have sinned. Every person would have to die and go to the place the Bible calls Hell because of his or her sin, but God loves everyone in the whole world, and He has made a way for people to go to Heaven.

"This is the way to Heaven, Nicodemus: Believe in Me—Jesus—to save you from your sins. God loved you so much that He sent Me, His only Son, to die for your sins so you wouldn't have to. Whoever believes in Me will not have to go to Hell when he dies, but he will live forever and ever and ever in a beautiful, perfect place called Heaven.

"And, life in Heaven won't be like the life you know on Earth. In Heaven, there will be no sin. No one will steal or kill. No one will ever hurt another person. No one will do or say unkind things. There will be no pain, there will be no tears, and there will be no death.

"And now, Nicodemus, you know the truth. You know the way to have everlasting life. Believe in Me."

Teacher's Note

Everlasting: existing or continuing without end

John 14:6

> 6   Jesus saith unto him, I am the way, the truth, and the life: no man cometh unto the Father, but by me

APPLYING THE STORY

Most people are like Nicodemus. Most of us have thought that the way to go to Heaven is to do good things. Maybe we think that if we go to church and Sunday school, we will be able to go to Heaven when we die. Maybe we think that if we don't steal, we will go to Heaven when we die. Maybe we think that if we tell the truth, share, or obey our parents we will go to Heaven.

But, what did Jesus say is the way to Heaven? (Allow students to answer.) Jesus said we have to be born again. He also said that if we are not born again, we will not go to Heaven.

Then, He explained being born again. Our spirits—the part of us that can know God—are dead because of sin, and our spirits need to be born again. The way for our spirits to be born again, Jesus said, is to believe in Him to save us from our sin. That is the only way for us to be saved.

What about you? Have you been born again? Or are you, like Nicodemus, trusting in the good things you do to save yourself?

Remember how simple it was for the Israelite people, the Jews, to be saved from death when they had been bitten by the deadly snakes? All they had to do was believe God and look up at the brass snake. If they did so, they would live.

It's just the same for you to be saved from death and Hell. All you have to do is believe God and look up to Jesus, and trust in Him to save you.

God said He loved everyone in the world so much that He sent His only Son to save each person from their sin, death, and Hell. He said He gave His only Son to pay the price for our sin.

If you are wanting to trust Jesus as your Saviour, I will be glad to talk to you after class today. When you trust Him, you will be born again, and, like Jesus told Nicodemus, you will have everlasting life with Him in Heaven. And you will begin a whole new life as a Christian. Will you trust Him today?

Teaching Tip

Take a few moments here to share your testimony. Share what you believed about how to go to Heaven before you knew the truth. If you grew up hearing the true Gospel, and you never believed salvation came through works, share the testimony of someone else who believed salvation came through anything other than trusting Jesus. This will make it personal and relevant for your students.

Review Game/Questions

Candy Jeopardy

Materials Needed
Several different bite-size candies
Question cards from the Ministry Resource CD

Set up
Buy several bite-size candies (such as Snickers, Hershey Kisses, etc.). Print and cut out question cards. Tape the candies on the board. Underneath each candy, place three question cards—word side down.

Playing the Game
Call on a student to pick a card. For example, the student will say, "Hershey Kisses for two pieces." You will then pick the card under the Hershey Kisses that says two pieces. Read the question to the student. If the student answers correctly, that student receives the two Hershey Kisses.

1. What was the name of the ruler of the Jews in today's lesson?
   Answer: Nicodemus

2. When did Nicodemus go to Jesus?
   Answer: At night

3. How did Nicodemus and other religious leaders think they could get to Heaven?
   Answer: By being good

4. What did Jesus tell Nicodemus he had to do in order to go to Heaven?
   Answer: Be born again.

5. Did Nicodemus understand what Jesus said?
   Answer: No!

6. What did Nicodemus think Jesus meant by saying, "Ye must be born again"?
   Answer: Nicodemus thought Jesus was referring to a physical birth.

7. What type of birth was Jesus really referring to?
   Answer: A spiritual birth

8. What illustration did Jesus use to describe the spiritual birth?
   Answer: It is like the wind. You can't see it or understand how it works, but you know it is real.

9. In John 3:16, what did Jesus tell Nicodemus he needed to do to have eternal life?
   Answer: Believe in Him.

10. How can a person today be born again?
    Answer: By believing in Jesus

Teaching the Memory Verse

John 3:7

7   *Marvel not that I said unto thee, Ye must be born again.*

Jesus is talking to Nicodemus. Jesus tells Nicodemus "marvel not" which means don't be surprised that I say, you must have another birth. In order to be born again we must have a birth already. That would be the day we were born! Ask the students if they know their physical birthday. Of course they do. Jesus says we must have another birth as well. We need to have a spiritual birthday as well in order to spend eternity with God. We need to acknowledge that we are sinners, believe that Jesus died for our sins, and call upon the Lord to save us—then we will be born again!

Around we go again and again!

If the class is small enough, sit in a circle. Otherwise develop a pattern in which the students will respond in order (e.g., zigzag). The first student says the reference. The next student says, "marvel." The next says, "not," etc. Continue this pattern until all the words of the verse are said. Then start again with the next student and start with the reference. This time go faster. Continue again going even faster. Repeat several times.

Object Lesson—Invisible Wind

Materials Needed:
One balloon for each child

Lesson:
Hand one balloon to each child and have them blow the balloon up but not tie it. If you are teaching younger age children who cannot blow up their own balloons, purchase a manual balloon pump and use this to inflate the balloon. At the count of three have the children place their balloons on the floor and let go of them. There will be balloons flying all over the place. Have a worker collect the balloons and throw them away.

Ask the children, "What made the balloons fly around the room?" Ask them, "Did you see the air come out of the balloon?" You cannot see air, but you saw the effects of the air by it pushing the balloon around the room.

Application:
In John 3:8, Jesus told Nicodemus that he could hear the air but not see it. Jesus also told Nicodemus that you can see the working of the Holy Spirit but cannot see the Holy Spirit with your eyes. Ask the children, "Have you ever done something and felt bad about it?" If you are saved, that is the Holy Spirit working on your heart. The Holy Spirit was working on Nicodemus' life, and he didn't even see Him doing it.

Craft—"God So Loved" Ruler

Getting It Together

Paper
Glue
Crayons

Per student:
1   Ruler from Ministry Resouce CD
1   Globe from Ministry Resource CD

Putting It Together

1.   Print out ruler and globe for each student to color.
2.   Attach globe to the ruler.

Seeing It Together

Nicodemus was a ruler in his city. As each student makes a ruler, discuss how all men need to trust Jesus as Saviour to be born again. Encourage each student to tell the kids in his neighborhood about Jesus.

 # Additional Resources

Find the following items on the Ministry Resource CD:

•   Coloring Page (for younger children)

•   Activity Page (for older children)

•   Student Take-Home Paper

•   PowerPoint Presentation

Suggested Classroom Schedule

Before Class	Complete attendance record. Provide students with coloring pages/activity pages.
Opening	Welcome
Prayer	Prayer requests and praise reports from the children
Song Time	
Memory Verse	Psalm 86:5
Song Time	
Object Lesson	Quench Your Thirst
Bible Lesson	Jesus Meets the Samaritan Woman
Application/Invitation	Help saved students apply lesson. Invite unsaved students to receive Christ.
Snack	Ice Cream Cones with Yogurt
Review Game/ Questions	Sink or Swim
Craft	Mini Bucket
Closing	Give announcements and pray. Distribute take-home papers.

Lesson Ten Overview

Jesus Meets the Samaritan Woman

Theme— Jesus loves all people and can save anyone.

Scripture
John 4:4–29, 39

Memory Verse
Psalm 86:5—*"For thou, Lord, art good, and ready to forgive; and plenteous in mercy unto all them that call upon thee."*

Lesson Outline
Introducing the Story
In the story we will hear today, we will learn about a Samaritan woman that Jesus spoke to. The Jews hated the Samaritans and didn't understand why Jesus would talk to this woman. Jesus taught that no matter the background, race, or age everyone needs the Gospel.

Telling the Story
1. **Jesus Journeys from Judaea to Galilee** *(vv.1–4, John 12:26)*
2. **Jesus Rests from His Journey** *(vv. 6, 8, Luke 23, 34)*
3. **Jesus Meets a Samaritan Woman** *(vv. 7, 9) —Flash Card 10.1*
4. **Jesus and the Woman Talk** *(vv. 10–14)*
5. **The Woman Still Thinks about Earthly Water** *(v. 15)*
6. **Jesus Knows All about the Woman** *(vv. 16–18, Hebrews 4:13, Romans 3:20)*
7. **Jesus Reveals Himself as the Messiah** *(vv. 19–26) —Flash Card 10.7*
8. **The Woman Shares the Gospel** *(vv. 25–29, Romans 11:33, Psalm 66:16)—Flash Card 10.8*
9. **The Samaritan People Believe in Jesus** *(v. 39)*

Applying the Story
Jesus' love and salvation is for every person, everywhere!

10 Lesson Ten

Jesus Meets the Samaritan Woman

Theme: Jesus loves all people and can save anyone.

Scripture

John 4:4–29, 39

4 And he must needs go through Samaria.

5 Then cometh he to a city of Samaria, which is called Sychar, near to the parcel of ground that Jacob gave to his son Joseph.

6 Now Jacob's well was there. Jesus therefore, being wearied with his journey, sat thus on the well: and it was about the sixth hour.

7 There cometh a woman of Samaria to draw water: Jesus saith unto her, Give me to drink.

8 (For his disciples were gone away unto the city to buy meat.)

9 Then saith the woman of Samaria unto him, How is it that thou, being a Jew, askest drink of me, which am a woman of Samaria? for the Jews have no dealings with the Samaritans.

10 Jesus answered and said unto her, If thou knewest the gift of God, and who it is that saith to thee, Give me to drink; thou wouldest have asked of him, and he would have given thee living water.

11 The woman saith unto him, Sir, thou hast nothing to draw with, and the well is deep: from whence then hast thou that living water?

12 Art thou greater than our father Jacob, which gave us the well, and drank thereof himself, and his children, and his cattle?

13 Jesus answered and said unto her, Whosoever drinketh of this water shall thirst again:

14 But whosoever drinketh of the water that I shall give him shall never thirst; but the water that I shall give him shall be in him a well of water springing up into everlasting life.

15 The woman saith unto him, Sir, give me this water, that I thirst not, neither come hither to draw.

16 Jesus saith unto her, Go, call thy husband, and come hither.

Memory Verse

Psalm 86:5
"For thou, Lord, art good, and ready to forgive; and plenteous in mercy unto all them that call upon thee."

Snack Suggestion

Yogurt Ice Cream Cones
To help the students remember today's lesson, prepare small ice cream cone cups to be used with blue yogurt (to represent water).

17 The woman answered and said, I have no husband. Jesus said unto her, Thou hast well said, I have no husband:

18 For thou hast had five husbands; and he whom thou now hast is not thy husband: in that saidst thou truly.

19 The woman saith unto him, Sir, I perceive that thou art a prophet.

20 Our fathers worshipped in this mountain; and ye say, that in Jerusalem is the place where men ought to worship.

21 Jesus saith unto her, Woman, believe me, the hour cometh, when ye shall neither in this mountain, nor yet at Jerusalem, worship the Father.

22 Ye worship ye know not what: we know what we worship: for salvation is of the Jews.

23 But the hour cometh, and now is, when the true worshippers shall worship the Father in spirit and in truth: for the Father seeketh such to worship him.

24 God is a Spirit: and they that worship him must worship him in spirit and in truth.

25 The woman saith unto him, I know that Messias cometh, which is called Christ: when he is come, he will tell us all things.

26 Jesus saith unto her, I that speak unto thee am he.

27 And upon this came his disciples, and marvelled that he talked with the woman: yet no man said, What seekest thou? or, Why talkest thou with her?

28 The woman then left her waterpot, and went her way into the city, and saith to the men,

29 Come, see a man, which told me all things that ever I did: is not this the Christ?

39 And many of the Samaritans of that city believed on him for the saying of the woman, which testified, He told me all that ever I did.

Teacher's Checklist

- ❑ Read John 4:4–29, 39 daily.
- ❑ Study Lesson Ten.
- ❑ Flash cards 10.1–10.3
- ❑ Prepare snack—Yogurt and ice cream cones.
- ❑ Print flash cards for memory verse from the Ministry Resource CD.
- ❑ Gather for object lesson—bottle of water.
- ❑ Purchase for craft—pipe cleaner and styrofoam cup (one per student).
- ❑ Gather for craft—crayons.
- ❑ Print for craft—verse template from the Ministry Resource CD.
- ❑ Print and duplicate Coloring Pages or Activity Pages on the Ministry Resource CD (one per student).
- ❑ Print and duplicate Take-Home Paper on the Ministry Resource CD (one per student).

Bible Lesson

Scripture: John 4:4–29, 39

INTRODUCING THE STORY

What is your very favorite color? (Allow students to answer.) What is your very least favorite color? (Again, allow time for answers.) We all have favorites and least favorites of colors, foods, types of clothing, subjects in school, hobbies, and many other things. Sometimes we don't know exactly why we like or don't like something, but for some reason or another, we just like it or don't like it.

Sometimes we have dislikes for certain people. Now, that's a very sad thing, disliking people. Do you know why it is sad to dislike people? (Wait for answers.) It is sad to dislike people because God made every person, He loves every person, and He wants us to show His love to every person.

We may not know why we don't like people—sometimes we just don't like one particular thing about a person, and so we don't like that person.

Let me explain. Someone might not like handicapped people, because they feel uncomfortable around handicapped people. The person doesn't know why the handicapped person looks or acts the way he or she does, and so, that person doesn't know how to act around the handicapped person. And they just decide they don't like handicapped people, because that's easier than trying to learn more about handicapped people and how to be helpful to them.

Someone else might not like people who have more money than he or she does. Maybe he thinks people with more money think they are better than others, or maybe he thinks rich people are proud. Sometimes a wealthy (rich) person doesn't like people who don't have much money. He may feel uncomfortable around them, and so it's easier just to decide he doesn't like them, rather than learning about them and getting to know them.

Some people don't like anyone who has a different color of skin than they have. Or they may not like people of just one particular skin color. Now, of course, they don't know all the people of that skin color, but for one reason or another they have decided to dislike and stay away from every person who has that color of skin.

There are other reasons people don't like someone before they even get to know them:

- Girls might dislike all boys.

- Boys might dislike all girls.
- People without glasses might dislike people who wear glasses.
- Someone might dislike others because of the clothes they wear.
- People might not like someone else based on his or her weight.
- Some people don't like those of a different nationality or religion than theirs.

In the days when Jesus was on Earth, the Jews (the people of Jesus' nationality) didn't like a certain group of people—the Samaritans. They didn't like them simply because they were not Jews—well, they were half Jew and half other nationalities. The Jews thought they were better than the Samaritans. The Jews hated the Samaritans so much that when they traveled from the Jewish land of Judaea to the Jewish land of Galilee, they refused to go through the land of Samaria where the Samaritans lived. Even though the shortest path would have been to go through Samaria, the Jews journeyed many miles out of their way so they wouldn't have to go through Samaria.

So, we see that even back in Jesus' time on Earth, people disliked other groups of people. And, just like today, these dislikes, or prejudices, are not based on really knowing the person. Do you ever wonder if Jesus had prejudices against certain groups of people? Let's listen to today's true story from the Bible to learn the answer to that question.

Teaching Tip

Using a map of the land of Palestine, show your class the direct route, through Palestine, from Judaea to Galilee. Then show them the route the Jews usually took, going east, crossing the Jordan River, then going north to bypass Samaria, and, finally, going back west to Galilee. The Jews would rather travel twice the necessary distance than to have contact with the Samaritans.
Refer to the map throughout the lesson.

THE STORY

1. Jesus Journeys from Judaea to Galilee (vv. 1–4)

Jesus had been preaching, teaching, and performing miracles in Judaea, and the time came for Him and His disciples to return to Galilee.

Jesus and His disciples didn't travel by car, SUV, train, bus, or plane. They usually didn't even travel on horseback. When Jesus wanted to go somewhere, He almost always walked—just like everyone else in His time. In fact, there were no cars, buses, trains, or planes, and so people had to walk when they wanted to go somewhere.

"Okay, men, we'll pick up our belongings and head out for Galilee first thing in the morning," Jesus told His disciples.

"Let's see, that journey will be a little over a hundred miles, so we should get to Galilee in four or five days," Peter said to himself.

But Peter was surprised when he heard what Jesus said next: "And, we're not going the usual route. I need to go through Samaria. It's a much shorter journey, going through Samaria, you know; and I need to take care of some things along the way. Yes, I need to go through Samaria."

"What?" the disciples were shocked. "We've never gone through Samaria. Doesn't Jesus remember that all Jews hate the Samaritan people?!"

The disciples didn't want to go through Samaria. If it were up to them, they would never have gone through Samaria. But they reminded themselves of a decision each of them had made not very much earlier. Each of those twelve men had decided to follow Jesus—to be His disciple. They had purposed in their hearts to go where Jesus went, to do what Jesus did, and to love what Jesus loved. And they had decided to serve Him. So, although none of the disciples wanted to go through Samaria, they trusted that Jesus knew best; and they followed Him straight into the land of the people they hated.

John 12:26

26   *If any man serve me, let him follow me; and where I am, there shall also my servant be: if any man serve me, him will my Father honour.*

2. Jesus Rests from His Journey (v. 6, 8)

"Hey, it's past lunchtime, and we'd better go buy something to eat," one of the disciples said, as they came near to the Samaritan city of Sychar.

"Yeah," said another. "Let's all go into this city to buy some food."

"I tell you what," Jesus said, "you men go ahead, and I'll rest here on this well while you're gone."

"Are You sure, Jesus? We don't want to leave You here alone," they said.

"I'm sure. My Father led Me here because He had a work for me to do, and I need to be right here, at this well."

"Well, if You're sure, we'll go, and we'll get plenty of food to bring some back for You." And off the disciples went to the city.

Jesus was tired from the journey, and He was glad to sit on the well to rest. It was about noon, and they had been traveling all day. "This is a special well," Jesus thought, as He enjoyed the pleasant feeling of the sun warming His back. "This well belonged to Jacob, our Jewish ancestor, almost two thousand years ago—and it's still here. In fact, Jacob's grandfather, Abraham, was the first Jew—he was called the father of the Jews. Jacob would have been my great, great, great (36 greats in all) grandpa on Joseph's side, and I'm here, today, sitting on the exact well that he dug!"

Luke 3:23, 34

23   *And Jesus himself began to be about thirty years of age, being (as was supposed) the son of Joseph, which was the son of Heli....*

34   *Which was the son of Jacob, which was the son of Isaac, which was the son of Abraham, which was the son of Thara, which was the son of Nachor,*

As Jesus rested alone on the well, He thought about the Samaritan woman who, Jesus knew, would be coming soon to draw water out of the well. She needed to know that Jesus had come to save her from her sins. She was the reason Jesus needed to travel through Samaria. She needed to trust Jesus.

Jesus also thought about how good it would feel to drink a cold, refreshing cup of water. The sun was shining hotter now, and He was not only tired, but He was thirsty as well. And, here He was at a well full of water, but He didn't have anything to use to lower into the deep well to scoop out water for drinking.

3. Jesus Meets a Samaritan Woman (vv. 7, 9)

Flash Card 10.1

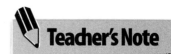

Teacher's Note

Draw: to pull up or out; to raise from any depth; as, in this case, to draw water from a well.

And there Jesus sat on Jacob's well, waiting for the Samaritan woman to come to get water out of the well. He knew He would ask her for a drink of water, and He knew what He was going to teach her about water.

Soon, the Samaritan woman came to the well, carrying a pitcher with which to draw water out of the well. It had been a tiring walk over the rugged path, and she was hot and tired.

And the kindest man who ever lived looked into the eyes of the Samaritan woman—a woman whom the rest of the Jews hated and called dirty—and He asked her for a drink of water.

"I can't believe this," said the Samaritan woman. "You're a Jew, and You're asking me—a Samaritan woman—for a drink of water? I have never, in my whole life, been spoken to by a Jew. The Jews don't do anything with the

Samaritans—they don't help us when we're in trouble, they don't look at us, and they never talk to us. So, why are You asking me for a drink?"

4. Jesus and the Woman Talk (vv. 10–14)

Those same kind eyes looked into the woman's eyes as Jesus said, "If you knew the wonderful gift God has for you, and if you knew who it is that has asked you for a drink of water, you would have asked Me for living water."

The woman wondered about what Jesus had said. "A gift from God?" she asked herself. "And, who is this man who says He has living water?"

She spoke to Jesus, "Sir, You don't have a pitcher or anything to get water out of the well, and this well is very deep. So, where would You get this living water?

"Do You think You're better than our great, great, (36 greats) grandfather Jacob—the one who gave us the well? Why, Jacob built this well. Jacob even drank out of this well himself; and his children and his cattle drank out of the well, too. You don't think You can give me any better water than Jacob has given us through this well, do You? You don't think you are better than Jacob, do You?"

Now, Jesus often used everyday things people did understand to explain spiritual truths people didn't understand. And that is what He did with water in this story. He used water to teach the woman about eternal life.

His answer to the woman was not at all what she expected. Jesus said, "whoever drinks out of Jacob's well, or any other well of water, will drink, and then he or she won't be thirsty—for awhile. But, soon, he or she will get thirsty and need another drink of water. That's the way it is with water. You get thirsty, you drink, you are not thirsty for awhile, you get thirsty again, you drink again…. It's like a circle that never ends.

"But I have different water to give. It's living water. It is water that God puts inside a person, and it stays in him or her forever. Here you have springs of water that bubble up from the ground, and the water just keeps bubbling up out of the spring and never stops. How would you like to have a spring of water—water of life—inside you that just keeps bubbling up and never stops?"

5. The Woman Still Thinks About Earthly Water (v. 15)

The woman didn't understand about eternal life or about living water. She thought Jesus was talking about water she could take home in her waterpot that would make it so she would never again have to make the long, hot trip to the well to get water for her family. She wanted this water that she thought would make her life easier. She didn't know that Jesus was talking about eternal life that would change her whole life forever. She didn't know that what Jesus was talking about would make her life better than she had ever dreamed and would provide for her a home in Heaven as well. She said to Jesus, "Sir, give me this water, so I will never be thirsty, and I won't have to come back to this well ever again."

6. Jesus Knows All About the Woman (vv. 16–18)

Jesus could see that the Samaritan woman didn't understand. He could see that the woman wasn't thinking of herself as a sinner who needed to be saved from her sins. Jesus knew that before she could be saved from her sins, she needed to realize in her heart that she was a sinner.

And Jesus knew exactly how to speak to her heart, reminding her that she was, indeed, a sinner. "I tell you what," said Jesus. "You go get your husband and bring him back to Me, and I will explain all of this to both of you."

"Well, Sir, I don't have a husband," the woman said. She sounded a little like she was trying to hide something.

"You're right," Jesus answered gently. "You don't have a husband. But you have had five husbands. You are living with a man now, and you aren't even married to him. So, what you said was true—you don't have a husband right now."

Hebrews 4:13

13 *Neither is there any creature that is not manifest in his sight: but all things are naked and opened unto the eyes of him with whom we have to do.*

The woman knew Jesus was telling the truth, and she was amazed that Jesus knew about her life—that Jesus even knew about her sin. Here she was, a woman of Samaria, hated by the Jews; and she was a sinful woman at

Teaching Tip

Draw a circle on the board or on a poster.

At the top of the circle, write "Get Thirsty." Then, about where the 4 would be on a clock, write "Drink Water." At the location of 8 on a clock, write "Thirst Quenched" or "Not Thirsty." Show students how they will soon be thirsty again, drink water again, have their thirst quenched, get thirsty again, etc., tracing around the circle with your finger as you explain.

Then, below the drawing of the circle, write "LIVING WATER." Draw a line under it, and explain that there is no circle for living water. You drink it once, and you never need any more. It's forever!

that. And here was this godly Jew talking to her. He knew about her sin, and yet, He spoke more kindly to her than anyone had ever spoken to her in her whole life. The woman began to feel ashamed of her sin.

Romans 3:20

20   *Therefore by the deeds of the law there shall no flesh be justified in his sight: for by the law is the knowledge of sin.*

Flash Card 10.2

7. Jesus Reveals Himself as the Messiah (vv. 19–26)

The woman said to Jesus, "Sir, I can see that You have great understanding from God."

As she spoke to Jesus, she began to want to hide her sin. She wanted to talk about something else, so she wouldn't have to think about or talk about her sin. She wanted to get Jesus talking about a different subject. "We Samaritans worship God here on this mountain," she said to Jesus. "But the Jews say that Jerusalem is the place where people should worship God."

Jesus didn't let her get Him off the subject. "It's not where a person worships," Jesus answered. "It's what is in a person's heart. God wants each person to worship Him from an honest heart that loves God."

"Hmm," the woman thought, "He may be right—I mean, He did know all about me and about my sin. I don't really want to think about this right now though. Someday the Messiah, the Saviour of the world, will come, and I'll learn about this from Him."

She turned to Jesus and said, "Well, I know that someday the Messiah is going to come. When He comes, He'll explain all of this to us. Then we won't have to wonder. We'll understand it all then. I'll just wait for Him"

Jesus turned His honest and loving eyes toward the woman again. His voice was gentle and strong at the same time. "I am the Messiah you have been waiting for. I have told you the truth. You don't have to wonder anymore. If you ask Me, I will give you the living water of eternal life."

Flash Card 10.3

8. The Woman Shares the Gospel (vv. 25–29)

As soon as Jesus had told the woman that He was the Messiah, the disciples returned with His lunch. They were amazed, and disappointed, that Jesus was talking with a woman—and a Samaritan woman at that! They knew

Jesus could do whatever He wanted, and they knew He would always do what was right, but still, they didn't understand why Jesus would be talking with a woman from a nation that all the Jews hated. They decided not to say anything to Him about it, though, because they knew Jesus was always right, even if they didn't understand.

Romans 11:33

33　O the depth of the riches both of the wisdom and
　　knowledge of God! how unsearchable are his judgments,
　　and his ways past finding out!

The woman believed that what Jesus had said was true. She believed He was the Messiah and that she was a sinner who needed to be forgiven by Him. She believed in Him to give her eternal life. She was excited. She was so excited, in fact, that she didn't even think about the water for which she had gone to the well. She just left her waterpot right where it was, beside the well, and she ran to the city.

In the city she found first one man, and then another. "You won't believe it!" she exclaimed, her heart full of joy. "I have found the Messiah! He knew all about my life, and my sin—and I hadn't even said one word about myself to Him. He told me all about myself. And, even though He knew all about me, He loved me! He loved me more than any person in this whole world has ever loved me! And now, I love Him. This really is the Christ. Come and meet Him for yourself. I know you will believe in Him and love Him, too!"

Psalm 66:16

16　Come and hear, all ye that fear God, and I will declare what
　　he hath done for my soul.

9. The Samaritan People Believe in Jesus (v. 39)

The woman, who hadn't understood Jesus' words at first, was now full of understanding. She was now born again, just as Jesus had talked about in our last story—the story of Nicodemus. The Samaritan woman's spirit was born again, and now her spirit had an understanding of the truths of God.

All the people to whom she spoke in the city saw that she was different. They saw that her eyes were full of peace and joy and happiness—it was as though she had living water bubbling up inside her! They knew God had changed her, and they wanted what she now had. The woman told them about Jesus and the living water, and they believed in Jesus, too!

APPLYING THE STORY

Isn't it wonderful that Jesus' love and salvation is for every person, everywhere? Isn't it wonderful that Jesus loves everyone?

Just think, if Jesus had hated the Samaritans, as the rest of the Jews hated them, the woman of Samaria never could have gotten saved. And the other Samaritan people couldn't have gotten saved either.

Or, think about this: What if Jesus did love the Samaritans as He does, and the Samaritan woman trusted Him as she did, but the Samaritan woman hated the rest of the Samaritans? If she hated them because she didn't like the clothes they wore or because she was poor and they were rich or for some other reason, she wouldn't have told the Samaritan men about Jesus, and they wouldn't have gotten saved.

That's why God wants us to love every person. He doesn't want us to dislike groups of people; but, rather, He wants us to want to share with everyone what He did for us and for them when He died on the cross to pay for our sins.

John 15:12

12   This is my commandment, That ye love one another, as I have loved you.

Romans 13:8

8   Owe no man any thing, but to love one another: for he that loveth another hath fulfilled the law.

Jesus' love and salvation from sin is for every person in the world. Jesus' love and salvation doesn't depend on our nationality, how rich or poor we are, the color of our skin, how we dress, our size, whether we are a boy or a girl—it doesn't depend on anything! Jesus loves everyone, and He came to save from his or her sin every person who trusts in Him.

John 3:16

16   For God so loved the world, that he gave his only begotten Son, that whosoever believeth in him should not perish, but have everlasting life.

What about you? Do you love all people? Do you want to share with everyone what Jesus did for you, when you trusted Him as your Saviour? Or, are there some people you don't like, and you don't want to tell them about Jesus?

If that is the case with you, God wants to change your hatred or your dislike into love! If you tell God that you don't like certain people or a certain group of people, and that you want to love them like He does—if you tell Him you are giving your hatred to Him and you want Him to put His love inside you in the place of hatred or dislike—He will!

If you have not trusted in Jesus to save you, you can do it today! You can be born again, as Jesus told Nicodemus in our story last week. You can have the living water inside you, as Jesus told the Samaritan woman in this week's story. You can have eternal life—a home in Heaven forever.

And when Jesus saves us, He changes us! He fills us with a well of water bubbling up inside us. It's not water we can drink, but it stays in our hearts, filling us with peace and joy and happiness—and everlasting life. Everlasting means "forever." Once we have trusted Jesus, He will never take our everlasting life away.

And people will see the change Jesus makes in your life. They will see He has given you love you didn't have before, as you speak kindly to others and show care for them. They will see the happiness deep in your heart, as you have a brighter smile than before. They will see your heart is more peaceful than it was before. They will see that Jesus is making you more patient, as they see you play with your little brother or sister. They will see your gentleness as you help older people. They will see He has given you new life.

Galatians 5:22–23

22   But the fruit of the Spirit is love, joy, peace, longsuffering, gentleness, goodness, faith,

23   Meekness, temperance: against such there is no law.

They will see the changes in your life, and when you tell them that it is your faith and trust in Jesus that changed you, they will be interested to know how Jesus did that in your life.

And you can tell them—just like the Samaritan woman told the people in her village how Jesus had changed her life!

Teaching Tip

Be sure to share with your students that there are some groups of people who, although we should love them and want the best for them, we need to be wise in our dealings with them. This would include strangers they meet when they are not under the protection of their parents' presence. It would also include people the Bible warns us to avoid, such as a foolish person.

Proverbs 14:7—*Go from the presence of a foolish man, when thou perceivest not in him the lips of knowledge.*

Proverbs 13:20—*He that walketh with wise men shall be wise: but a companion of fools shall be destroyed.*

We want our students to understand the importance of being protected by their God-ordained authorities, even as they allow God to increase their love for all people.

Review Game/Questions

Sink or Swim

Materials Needed
None

Playing the Game

Divide the class into two teams. Line up the two teams in two lines across the room facing each other.

Ask a student on Team 1 a question. If the student answers correctly he can sink someone on Team 2 (have student sit down). Then ask a student on Team 2 a question. If the student answers correctly he can either sink someone on Team 1 or rescue one of his "sunken" team members (a seated student can stand back up and play the game). The winning team is the team with the most students standing.

1. When Jesus travelled from Judea to Galilee, what city did he decide to go through?
   Answer: Samaria

2. Did the disciples want to go through Samaria?
   Answer: No

3. Where did Jesus stop to rest on His journey through Samaria?
   Answer: A well/Jacob's well

4. What did Jesus ask the Samaritan woman who had come with a pitcher to the well?
   Answer: He asked her for a drink.

5. What kind of water did Jesus offer to the Samaritan woman?
   Answer: Living water

6. Did the Samaritan woman understand at first what Jesus meant by "living water"?
   Answer: No. She thought it was water she could put in her pitcher.

7. Did Jesus know all about the woman at the well? How do we know that?
   Answer: Yes. He knew all about her past and current relationships.

8. When Jesus told the woman at the well that He was indeed the Messiah, how did she respond in her heart?
    Answer: She believed!

9. After she believed in Jesus, what did the excited woman leave her water pots to do?
    Answer: She told everyone about Jesus.

10. To whom does Jesus give His love and salvation?
    Answer: To everyone! (Not just a certain group of people)

 # Teaching the Memory Verse

Psalm 86:5

5   *For thou, Lord, art good, and ready to forgive; and plenteous in mercy unto all them that call upon thee.*

Print the flash cards for Psalm 86:5 from the Ministry Resource CD. Laminate for durability.

The Lord sets the supreme example here for us to follow. Mercy means forgiveness shown toward someone whom it is within one's power to punish! Isn't that just like God? He definitely has the power to punish but He shows mercy instead. God is ready to forgive and show compassion. He doesn't make us earn forgiveness or pay for it. Are you always ready to forgive? Or, do you want the other person to hurt and suffer first before you forgive them? Let's be ready to forgive just like Jesus!

Object Lesson—Quench Your Thirst

Materials Needed:
Bottle of Water

Lesson:

Ask the children: How many of you are thirsty? After the class raises their hands, ask a child to come to the front and join you.

Do you know that your body is made up of 65–70% of water? Water is really important. What do you think would happen if you never drank water again? Your body can only last for up to three days without water. Someone name something that makes you thirsty. What happens when you drink water? The thirst goes away.

Application:

When you were born into this world you were born a sinner. This means that your soul was "thirsty" for something. There had to be something to take the thirst away. Jesus Christ is the only way that your soul will not thirst again. Jesus told the woman at the well, "Whosoever drinketh of the water that I shall give him shall never thirst." Jesus Christ washes the sin away from your sinful heart.

How many of you think if (chosen student) drinks this bottle of water he will be thirsty again? Yes! You're right. He will thirst again physically. If you trust Christ as your Saviour, He will wash your sins away and you will never thirst again spiritually.

Craft—Mini Bucket

Getting It Together

Crayons

Per student:
1   Styrofoam cup
1   Pipe cleaner
1   Verse template from the Ministry
     Resource CD

Putting It Together

1. Using crayons, have each student color a styrofoam cup.
2. Add a pipe cleaner for a handle.
3. Print out verse from Ministry Resource CD and put inside the "bucket."

Seeing It Together

Jesus loves all people! As the students prepare their buckets, talk about the woman who came to get a drink of water and found Jesus. God is preparing people's hearts and wants to use each student to draw people to Jesus for salvation.

 # Additional Resources

Find the following items on the Ministry Resource CD:

•   Coloring Page (for younger children)

•   Activity Page (for older children)

•   Student Take-Home Paper

•   PowerPoint Presentation

Suggested Classroom Schedule

Before Class		Complete attendance record. Provide students with coloring pages/activity pages.
Opening		Welcome
Prayer		Prayer requests and praise reports from the children
Song Time		
Memory Verse		Matthew 5:16
Song Time		
Object Lesson		This Little Light of Mine
Bible Lesson		Jesus Preaches a Sermon
Application/Invitation		Help saved students apply lesson. Invite unsaved students to receive Christ.
Snack		Cereal Snack Mix
Review Game/ Questions		Left or Right
Craft		Lightbulb Keychain
Closing		Give announcements and pray. Distribute take-home papers.

Lesson Eleven Overview

Jesus Preaches a Sermon
Theme—Jesus gives us instructions for living.

Scripture
Matthew 5:1–16

Memory Verse
Matthew 5:16—"*Let your light so shine before men, that they may see your good works, and glorify your Father which is in heaven.*"

Lesson Outline

Introducing the Story
Living the Christian life is much like climbing a mountain. In Jesus' lesson, He taught the multitudes how to begin at the bottom of the mountain of the Christian life and climb higher and higher in our relationships with Him.

Telling the Story
1. **Jesus Prepares to Speak to the Multitudes** (vv. 1–2) —*Flash Card 11.1*
2. **Blessed Are the Poor in Spirit** (v. 3)—*Flash Card 11.2*
3. **Blessed Are They That Mourn** (v. 4)
4. **Blessed Are the Meek** (v. 5, Matthew 11:28–29)
5. **Blessed Are They Which Do Hunger and Thirst after Righteousness** (v. 6, Psalm 42:1–2a, Psalm 63:1)
6. **Blessed Are the Merciful** (v. 7, Psalm 145:8)
7. **Blessed Are the Pure in Heart** (v. 8, 1 Timothy 1:5, Psalm 24:3–4)
8. **Blessed Are the Peacemakers** (v. 9, Psalm 119:165, Colossians 1:20a, 2 Corinthians 1:18)
9. **Blessed Are the Persecuted** (vv. 10–12, John 14:6a)
10. **You Are the Salt of the Earth** (v. 13)
11. **You Are the Light of the World** (vv. 14–16)—*Flash Card 11.3*

Applying the Story
The Christian life is a step by step walk. You will grow to know Jesus better, and He will give you a deep happiness that no one else can give.

11 Lesson Eleven

Jesus Preaches a Sermon

Theme: Jesus gives us instructions for living.

Scripture

Matthew 5:1–16

1   And seeing the multitudes, he went up into a mountain: and when he was set, his disciples came unto him:

2   And he opened his mouth, and taught them, saying,

3   Blessed are the poor in spirit: for theirs is the kingdom of heaven.

4   Blessed are they that mourn: for they shall be comforted.

5   Blessed are the meek: for they shall inherit the earth.

6   Blessed are they which do hunger and thirst after righteousness: for they shall be filled.

7   Blessed are the merciful: for they shall obtain mercy.

8   Blessed are the pure in heart: for they shall see God.

9   Blessed are the peacemakers: for they shall be called the children of God.

10   Blessed are they which are persecuted for righteousness' sake: for theirs is the kingdom of heaven.

11   Blessed are ye, when men shall revile you, and persecute you, and shall say all manner of evil against you falsely, for my sake.

12   Rejoice, and be exceeding glad: for great is your reward in heaven: for so persecuted they the prophets which were before you.

13   Ye are the salt of the earth: but if the salt have lost his savour, wherewith shall it be salted? it is thenceforth good for nothing, but to be cast out, and to be trodden under foot of men.

14   Ye are the light of the world. A city that is set on an hill cannot be hid.

15   Neither do men light a candle, and put it under a bushel, but on a candlestick; and it giveth light unto all that are in the house.

16   Let your light so shine before men, that they may see your good works, and glorify your Father which is in heaven.

Snack Suggestion

Cereal Snack Mix
Give each child a bag and have them follow instructions to assemble their own snack mix. Instruct each child to scoop one spoonful of each of the following into their bag: cereal, m&ms, pretzel stix, and mini marshmallows.

✓ Teacher's Checklist

- ❑ Read Matthew 5:1–16 daily.
- ❑ Study Lesson Eleven.
- ❑ Flash cards 11.1–11.3
- ❑ Prepare snack—Cereal Snack Mix.
- ❑ Print and cut out "Left or Right" review game from the Ministry Resource CD.
- ❑ Print memory verse flash card from the Ministry Resource CD.
- ❑ Gather for memory verse—flashlight.
- ❑ Gather for object lesson—flashlight, picture of lighthouse.
- ❑ Print for craft—lightbulb template from the Ministry Resource CD.
- ❑ Purchase for craft—keychain.
- ❑ Gather for craft—scissors and hole punch.
- ❑ Print and duplicate Coloring Pages or Activity Pages on the Ministry Resource CD (one per student).
- ❑ Print and duplicate Take-Home Paper on the Ministry Resource CD (one per student).

   The Steps of Our Saviour | © 2011 Striving Together Publications

Bible Lesson

Scripture: Matthew 5:1–16

INTRODUCING THE STORY

Have you ever climbed a mountain? Or do you know someone who has climbed a high mountain? People who live in the mountains and who live in places where they do not have cars climb mountains because they need to get to places—to work, to church, to school, or anywhere they need to go.

Many people, though, climb mountains just for the fun of getting to the top. The very highest mountain in the world is Mount Everest, which is 29,035 feet tall. Mount Everest is in Asia, and many people go to Asia every year just for the purpose of climbing Mount Everest.

The highest mountain in our country—the United States of America—is Mount McKinley in Alaska. Mount McKinley is 20,320 feet tall, and many people go to Alaska every year just for the purpose of climbing Mount McKinley.

Whatever mountain a person climbs—Mount Everest in Asia, Mount McKinley in Alaska, or any other mountain—one thing is certain: they need to start at the bottom of the mountain and go step by step up to the top of the mountain.

Some mountains are not very high, and they are easy to climb. Others, like Mount Everest and Mount McKinley, are several miles high, and they are very difficult to climb. But for each mountain you climb, remember, you will never get to the top unless you begin at the bottom (the base).

Jesus climbed a mountain. It wasn't an extremely high mountain like Mount Everest, and He didn't climb it just for fun. Jesus climbed a mountain in order to teach a huge group of people—the Bible calls it a multitude of people—a lesson His Heavenly Father wanted Him to teach.

As we listen to Jesus' lesson on the mountain, which many people call "The Sermon on the Mount," think about mountain climbing. Living the Christian life is much like climbing a mountain. We begin at the base (or bottom), which is trusting Jesus to save us from our sin. Then, we climb higher and higher, step by step, as we grow as Christians. In Jesus' lesson, He taught the multitudes (and us) how to begin at the bottom of the mountain of the Christian life and climb higher and higher in our relationship with Him.

Act It Out

Wear climbing-type boots or shoes, a visor or helmet, a headlamp (if possible), heavy gloves, a backpack, and a rope around your waist to represent a mountain climber. Carry a pickaxe, if possible. As you talk about mountain climbing, gently throw your rope as if to catch it on a higher rock for support and move your arms and legs as if you were on an extreme mountain climbing expedition.

THE STORY

Flash Card 11.1

1. Jesus Prepares to Speak to the Multitudes (vv. 1–2)

The people had just climbed a mountain. They had started at the beginning, down at the bottom of the mountain. Then they had climbed up the mountain, one step at a time. They couldn't take the second step before they had taken the first; they couldn't take the third step before they had taken the second, and they couldn't take the hundredth step before they had taken the ninety-ninth step.

So, there they were on the side of the mountain—Jesus, with His disciples gathered closely around Him—and a whole multitude of other people. Jesus looked at the people, and He began to teach them.

He was going to teach them how they could be really happy—deep-down-in-their-heart happy. In fact, the very first word that Jesus said when He began teaching was the word *blessed*. This word means "happy." And it is talking about having a happiness and a joy down deep in your heart. It's talking about the kind of happiness that stays with you wherever you go, whatever happens to you. So what did Jesus say would make people happy like this? Listen closely.

Flash Card 11.2

2. Blessed Are the Poor in Spirit (v. 3)

Jesus said, "Blessed are the poor in spirit."

I can just imagine all the people listening and saying to themselves, "What?! People who are poor are happy?!"

These people had seen poor beggars. The beggars around Galilee, where they lived, were so poor they didn't have anything. They didn't have a house, they didn't have a donkey to ride, they didn't have food. They only had a few rags to wear. They didn't even have a job because most of them were blind or lame, and they couldn't work. If they didn't beg for food or money, they would starve to death.

The disciples and the other people shuddered as they thought about the beggars. And they said to themselves, "I'm sure glad I'm not a beggar." And the children thought, "I'm glad my daddy isn't blind or lame. I'm glad he can go to work to make a living for our family. I'm glad Daddy doesn't have to beg, and I'm glad I don't have to beg."

But Jesus had said, "Blessed [or happy] are the poor in spirit." The people were confused. What did Jesus mean? Why would happiness come from

Teacher's Note

Blessed: happy; prosperous; enjoying spiritual happiness and the favor of God

being like a beggar? They thought, "That wouldn't make me happy—that would make me miserable!"

But then the people realized that Jesus said, "Blessed are the poor in spirit." You see, he wasn't talking about being poor on the outside. Being rich or poor on the outside has nothing to do with how happy you can be on the inside. Jesus was talking about being poor on the inside—in your spirit.

Think for a minute about the beggars. Picture a man sitting by the side of the road, wrapped in dirty rags, looking up at you as he holds up his cup to you. He calls out, "Please, will you give a coin to a poor beggar?"

Just like a beggar is dependent on others for what he needs on the outside, Jesus was telling us that we need to be dependent on God for what we need on the inside.

Think of how you feel on the inside. Do you feel like you can take care of yourself? Do you like to think your own thoughts and do your own things and go your own way? Or do you feel like you need help from God? Do you want God to teach you how to think like He does and to show you where He wants you to go and what He wants you to do?

If you really, way down deep in your heart, believe you need God's help in everything, then you are like a beggar in your spirit. You will go to God for help. You will ask Him what He wants you to do, who He wants you to talk to, how He wants you to behave—you will ask Him for help in everything!

Being like a beggar on the inside is the only way a person can be saved from his or her sins. Remember, to be saved, a person needs to realize that there is nothing he can do to save himself from his sin, and he needs to believe in Jesus, knowing that Jesus has already paid the price for his salvation.

But it doesn't stop at salvation! In order to have real, deep-down-in-your-heart happiness, every Christian (every person who has trusted Jesus' death on the cross to pay for his or her sins) needs to have a humble heart, wanting God's help in every part of life. This makes you deep-down-in-your-heart happy.

That is the first step to climbing the mountain of the Christian life.

Teacher's Note

Humble: having a deep sense of unworthiness in the sight of God

3. Blessed Are They That Mourn (v. 4)

"There's something else that will make you blessed—deep-down-in-your-heart happy," Jesus said. "The next step up the mountain is to mourn, and when you mourn you will be blessed."

"When we mourn?!" the people silently asked themselves. "When a person mourns, that means he is full of sorrow. A person mourns over the death of someone he or she loves. A person mourns when something terrible has happened. How could mourning make us happy?"

Think about what causes God to mourn—He mourns about sin. In fact, sin is what has caused every single bad thing in this world. Sin is what brought death into the world, way back in the Garden of Eden. Sin is what causes people to kill and steal. Sin is what causes parents to not take care of their children like God wants them to. Sin is what causes people to drink and hurt each other. Sin is what causes people to be unkind to each other. Sin is why God had to send His Son to die on the cross—so Jesus could pay for our sin.

Jesus said, "When you mourn over what God mourns over, you will be comforted. God will comfort you. And you know that comfort from God will make you deep-down-in-your-heart happy. There can be no better comfort than the comfort your loving Heavenly Father gives you in your heart."

So when you sin, and when you see others sin, and you feel sorrow in your heart over that sin, God will comfort you.

And when you mourn because, although you want to be like Jesus, you know in your heart that you are not very much like Him, God will comfort you. And God's comfort will make you extremely happy inside.

4. Blessed Are the Meek (v. 5)

Let's see what Jesus taught the people is the next step to climbing the mountain of the Christian life.

"If you want to be deep-down-in-your-heart happy," Jesus continued, "you will take the next step. You will walk so closely with God that He will make you more and more like Himself—He will make you meek."

Matthew 11:28–29

28 *Come unto me, all ye that labour and are heavy laden, and I will give you rest.*

29 *Take my yoke upon you, and learn of me; for I am meek and lowly in heart: and ye shall find rest unto your souls.*

Meekness means you are willing to submit to God. It means you give up your own way and your own "rights" so you can please God and help other people.

That's what Jesus did. He gave up everything He had in Heaven—the worship of angels, ruling with God the Father, streets of gold, and all the riches and beauty—to come to earth as a baby and then die on the cross to pay for our sins. He trusted God the Father to do what was best, and that is what God wants us to do too—He wants us to trust Him. When we trust Him, giving up our own way so He can have His way in our lives, we will be blessed—deep-down-in-our-hearts happy!

5. Blessed Are They Which Do Hunger and Thirst after Righteousness (v. 6)

When you have started at the base of the mountain and climbed up step by step, you will find something new going on inside you. You will find you have become hungry and thirsty in your heart.

"Hmm," the people thought, "how can being hungry and thirsty make us blessed?"

"It's not hungering for food or thirsting for water that I am talking about," Jesus said. "You will be blessed—deep-down-in-your-heart happy—when your heart hungers and thirsts for righteousness. That means your heart hungers and thirsts for right things. It is when, from the bottom of your heart, you want to do right so much that you become very, very hungry—like someone who hasn't had food for days—to do right. You become very, very thirsty—like someone in the desert who hasn't had a drink of water for days—to do right."

Psalm 42:1–2a

1   *As the hart panteth after the water brooks, so panteth my soul after thee, O God.*

2a   *My soul thirsteth for God, for the living God….*

Psalm 63:1

1   *O God, thou art my God; early will I seek thee: my soul thirsteth for thee, my flesh longeth for thee in a dry and thirsty land, where no water is.*

As you hunger and thirst for righteousness, you will become deep-down-in-your-heart happy. This is because you will have a closer relationship with God than you have ever had before in your life. You will be wanting with

Teaching Tip

If a student questions the verse's saying it is Jesus who is meek, but the lesson is saying it is God who is meek, you have a perfect opportunity to reinforce the Deity of Christ. Remind the students that God is three Persons—God the Father, God the Son, and God the Holy Spirit—all are God.

all your heart what God wants—righteousness—and you will be extremely happy inside.

6. Blessed Are the Merciful (v. 7)

Let's continue our hike up the mountain of the Christian life.

"Blessed are the merciful," Jesus said, "for they shall obtain mercy."

Remember that God showed His mercy to you when He sent His Son to die for your sins so you wouldn't have to go to the Lake of Fire forever when you die. We deserve the Lake of Fire, but instead God gave His only Son to die in our place—that's mercy.

When you think about the mercy God has for you—the greatest mercy that has ever been shown—you will be able to be merciful to those who have done wrong to you. When someone lies about you, you will be able to show mercy to him or her because God shows mercy to you. When someone takes something that belongs to you and ruins it, you will be able to show mercy to him or her because God shows mercy to you. When someone speaks unkindly to you, you will be able to show mercy to him or her because God shows mercy to you.

Psalm 145:8

8   The LORD is gracious, and full of compassion; slow to anger, and of great mercy.

"And then," Jesus said, "you will receive mercy as well, and you will be deep-down-in-your-heart happy!"

Teacher's Note

Mercy: that benevolence, mildness or tenderness of heart which disposes a person to overlook injuries, or to treat an offender better than he deserves; pity, compassion

7. Blessed Are the Pure in Heart (v. 8)

"Next," Jesus said, "the pure in heart will be blessed, for they shall see God."

"See God?" the people wondered. "How can we see God?"

A pure heart means that you want to please God because you love Him. It means you want to do those things that please God just because they please God—not because you are afraid you will get caught doing wrong; not because you are afraid of getting into trouble because you do wrong.

Being pure in heart means you don't just pretend to love God, but you really do love Him with all your heart.

1 Timothy 1:5

5   Now the end of the commandment is charity out of a pure
     heart, and of a good conscience, and of faith unfeigned.

When your heart is pure, you will be very close to God, and He will show more of Himself to you than He will to other people who don't have pure hearts. You will be very blessed—deep-down-in-your-heart happy!

Psalm 24:3–4

3   Who shall ascend into the hill of the Lord? or who shall
     stand in his holy place?
4   He that hath clean hands, and a pure heart; who hath not
     lifted up his soul unto vanity, nor sworn deceitfully.

8. Blessed Are the Peacemakers (v. 9)

"As you grow, you will become peacemakers," Jesus said, "and being peacemakers will make you deep-down-in-your-heart happy, as the whole world will notice that you are Christians—God's children."

Do you know what it means to be a peacemaker? It means you are someone who helps to make peace with others. We can be peacemakers as we choose not to argue when someone disagrees with us, as we don't try to get even with someone who wrongs us, as we don't gossip or spread unkind things about other people, and as we encourage others not to argue or fight. We get peace in our own hearts as we love and read the Bible.

Psalm 119:165

165 Great peace have they which love thy law: and nothing
      shall offend them.

There is another way we can be peacemakers, and it is a very exciting part of being a Christian—a child of God. We can be peacemakers by telling others about the Saviour, the Lord Jesus Christ. He died on the cross so we could all have peace with God. When someone trusts Jesus as his or her Saviour from sin, he gains peace with God, rather than his sin keeping him away from God, as it did before he was saved.

Colossians 1:20a

20a And, having made peace through the blood of his cross, by him to reconcile all things unto himself

2 Corinthians 1:18

18 And all things are of God, who hath reconciled us to himself by Jesus Christ, and hath given to us the ministry of reconciliation.

When you tell someone about Jesus' love for him and His death on the cross for his sins, you will be blessed—deep-down-in-your-heart happy. People will notice that you are like God, and you will be closer to God than ever!

Teacher's Note

Persecution: the infliction of pain, punishment or death upon others unjustly, particularly for adhering to a religious creed or mode of worship

9. Blessed Are the Persecuted (vv. 10–12)

As you climb up the mountain of the Christian life, you will not only have deep-down-in-your-heart happiness, but you will love God more than you could have imagined when you were still at the bottom. And, as you love God more and more, you will become more and more like Jesus.

When Jesus lived on this earth, many people treated Jesus unkindly. Many people called Jesus a liar, although we know that Jesus never lied. Jesus is the only person who never lied.

John 14:6a

6a Jesus saith unto him, I am the way, the truth, and the life

Although Jesus never lied, people lied about Him. They said He wasn't God's Son, although we know He was. They said He was from Satan, although we know He wasn't. They also tried to kill Jesus, and they said cruel things to Him.

Jesus was persecuted when He was on Earth—He was persecuted for doing right! And He told the people on the mountain that day, "Blessed are they which are persecuted for righteousness' sake—those who are treated wrongly because they do right."

"How could persecution—cruel treatment—bring us happiness?" the people wondered.

"When men speak hatefully to you, when they treat you cruelly because you are a Christian, and when they lie about you because of the good you do for Me—and not because you have done wrong—you will have a great reward in Heaven.

"They treated the preachers and prophets of long ago like that, too. Those preachers told the truth about God and His desire for the people to serve Him, but the people hated the truth, and so they hated the prophets, and they even killed many of them. But those prophets and preachers have a great reward in Heaven.

"When you are persecuted for doing right, be very, very glad in your heart. You will be very blessed now with deep-down-in-your-heart happiness, and you will be blessed in the future with great rewards in Heaven."

10. You Are the Salt of the Earth (v. 13)

"You are like salt," Jesus said. "Just like a little salt on your meat makes the meat taste better, Christians are here in this world to make things better. You are to take your deep-down-in-your-heart happiness wherever you go. And salt preserves meat—it keeps it from spoiling. Your presence in this world will keep the world from being a terrible place because you will tell others how they can have their sins forgiven."

11. You Are the Light of the World (vv. 14–16)

Flash Card 11.3

"The world is a dark place, full of sin," Jesus said. "But Christians are light in this dark world. Don't ever try to hide your light, for that light is the light of Christ.

"Hold your light up high, just like a tall lamp in your home, or a light that is mounted on the ceiling. When a light is held high, it spreads light to everything around it.

"When you let your light shine, it will light up all the good things you do for Me, and others will see your good deeds, and they will know that God is good. They will want to know God, too, when they see the good things you do for God.

"That will make you happy, and it will bring delight to Me, too."

APPLYING THE STORY

In His Sermon on the Mount, Jesus taught His disciples, and the whole multitude of people, how to grow as Christians.

He taught them that true blessing—deep-down-in-your-heart happiness—doesn't come from living your own way. It comes from living for God, in the way God planned for you to live.

You will be blessed if you are poor in spirit.

- Have you trusted in Jesus to forgive your sins, knowing that He is the only one who can forgive sin? Have you trusted His death on the cross to pay for your sins?
- If you have trusted Jesus to forgive your sins, do you live your life your own way, or do you have a humble heart, asking God to lead you in His way?

You will be blessed if you mourn.

- Do you feel sad in your heart when you sin, or do you sin without even thinking about the fact that your sin keeps you from having a happy relationship with God?
- Do you feel sad when you see other people sin, or do you not even notice sin?

You will be blessed if you are meek.

- Do you give up what you want, so you can have what God wants in your life?
- Do you choose God's way in the morning—reading your Bible, talking to God in prayer? Or do you just get up and go on with your day, not even thinking about God?

You will be blessed if you hunger and thirst after righteousness.

- Do you want to do right as much as you want to eat when you are hungry and to drink when you are thirsty?
- Do you choose to do right when you have a decision to make?

You will be blessed if you are merciful, pure in heart, and a peacemaker.

- Do you treat others better than they deserve (mercy), because that is how God treats you, or do you treat others unkindly when they treat you unkindly?

- Do you serve God because you love Him (a pure heart), or do you serve Him so others will think you are a good Christian?
- Do you tell others about Jesus so they can trust Him and have their sins forgiven (peacemaker)?

Are you willing to tell others you love Jesus even if they make fun of you or treat you unkindly? You can share your love for Jesus at school, the park, the store, and everywhere you go.

Are you "salt" in the world—do you make the world a better place by living for Jesus and loving others?

Do you let the light of Jesus shine through your life? Do others want to know Jesus because they see your light shining on the good things you do for Jesus?

The Christian life (the life after someone trusts Jesus as his or her Saviour) is often not an easy walk—it's not like a nice walk on a path through the park. It is a life that begins at the bottom of a mountain, and you have to walk up carefully, step by step. But as you take those steps, you will get to know Jesus better and better, and He will give you deep-down-in-your-heart happiness all along the way.

 **Review Game/Questions**

Left or Right

Materials Needed
Print Left and Right game from the Ministry Resource CD.

Set Up
Print and cut game from the Ministry Resource CD. Place the Left or Right cards in a pocket chart or on chalk tray.

Playing the Game
Divide the class into two teams. Ask a student a question. If he or she answers correctly, that student comes to the front and picks one card. Lift up the center square to reveal points. Now the student selects left or right. Lift up the square the student chooses. Give the points to the team name that was revealed. The team with the most points at the end of the game is the winner.

1. In today's story, what did Jesus teach the multitudes?
   Answer: He taught them how to be happy (blessed).

2. Name one of the groups of people Jesus said would be happy or blessed.
   Answer: To extend the review time, allow teams to take turns answering until all eight groups have been mentioned: the poor in spirit, those who mourn, the meek, those who are hungry and thirsty for righteousness, the merciful, the pure in heart, the peacemakers, and those who are persecuted.

3. What does God promise to do to those who mourn?
   Answer: He comforts them.

4. What does it mean to be meek?
   Answer: Meekness means you are willing to submit to God. It means to give up your own way.

5. Why are we able to show mercy to others?
   Answer: We can show mercy to others because God shows mercy to us.

6. If you want to truly see God and be close to Him, what type of heart should you have?
   Answer: A pure heart

7. What does it mean to be a peacemaker?
   Answer: It means you are someone who helps to make peace with others.

8. Why can you be happy if you are persecuted for doing what is right?
   Answer: Because God promises a reward for you in Heaven

9. At the end of His sermon, what two objects did Jesus compare Christians to?
   Answer: Salt and light

10. What is this special sermon often called?
    Answer: "The Sermon on the Mount"

Teaching the Memory Verse

Matthew 5:16

16 *Let your light so shine before men, that they may see your good works, and glorify your Father which is in heaven.*

Materials needed:
Flashlight

Place flash cards on the wall or write the verse on the board. Tell the students they will read from only the flash card that is lit. Turn off lights. Shine the light from the flashlight on the first flash card. After students have repeated the verse a few times, put the flashlight on flash card #2. Then back to flash card #1 and #2. Continue with the rest of the flash cards.

Object Lesson—This Little Light of Mine

Materials Needed:
Flashlight
Picture of lighthouse

Lesson:
Sing "This Little Light of Mine."

Application:
Ask the children, "What is the purpose of a flashlight? What about a lighthouse?" The lighthouse is set on a hill so the sailors can see it. The lighthouse warns of danger and also shows where the sailor should sail his ship safely. Jesus calls Christians the "light of the world." You have the choice of being a dim or bright light for the Lord Jesus. Don't be ashamed to be that light. It would be foolish for someone to cover the light of the lighthouse, and it would be foolish for a Christian to hide from living like a Christian. Shine brightly for Jesus.

 # Additional Resources

Find the following items on the Ministry Resource CD:

- Coloring Page (for younger children)
- Activity Page (for older children)
- Student Take-Home Paper
- PowerPoint Presentation

✂ Craft—Lightbulb Keychain

Getting It Together

Scissors
Hole punch (single hole punch)
Lightbulb template from the Ministry
   Resource CD

Per student:
1   Round keychain

Putting It Together

1.   Print out lightbulb and cut out.
2.   Punch a hole.
3.   Attach to keychain.

Seeing It Together

Jesus is the light to our path. He will show us what He wants as we read His Word each day.

Suggested Classroom Schedule

Before Class	Complete attendance record. Provide students with coloring pages/activity pages.	
Opening	Welcome	
Prayer	Prayer requests and praise reports from the children	
Song Time		
Memory Verse	Mark 12:30	
Song Time		
Object Lesson	Showing Jesus' Love	
Bible Lesson	A Woman Washes Jesus' Feet	
Application/Invitation	Help saved students apply lesson. Invite unsaved students to receive Christ.	
Snack	Fruit by the Foot	
Review Game/ Questions	Heart	
Craft	Kids Placemat	
Closing	Give announcements and pray. Distribute take-home papers.	

Lesson Twelve Overview

A Woman Washes Jesus' Feet
Theme—We should show our love to Jesus.

Scripture
Luke 7:36–50

Memory Verse
Mark 12:30—"And thou shalt love the Lord thy God with all thy heart, and with all thy soul, and with all thy mind, and with all thy strength: this is the first commandment."

Lesson Outline

Introducing the Story (Isaiah 55:8–9)
Today's story is about a woman who was considered in her town to be a sinful woman. Let's find out what Jesus thought about this woman who was known for her sin.

Telling the Story
1. **Jesus Goes to Dinner at Simon's House** (v. 36, Romans 16:16a)—Flash Card 12.1
2. **The Woman Washes Jesus' Feet and Anoints Him** (vv. 37–38))—Flash Card 12.2
3. **Simon Judges Jesus** (v. 39))—Flash Card 12.3
4. **Jesus Knows Simon's Thoughts** (v. 40)
5. **Jesus Tells a Story and Asks Simon a Question** (vv. 41–42)
6. **Simon's Answer to Jesus** (v. 43)
7. **Jesus Speaks of the Woman's Love** (vv. 44–48)
8. **The Guests Question Jesus' Credibility** (v. 49)
9. **Jesus Speaks to the Woman** (v. 50)

Applying the Story
Does your heart show your love for what Jesus has done for us?

12 Lesson Twelve

A Woman Washes Jesus' Feet

Theme: We should show our love to Jesus.

 ## Scripture

Luke 7:36–50

36 And one of the Pharisees desired him that he would eat with him. And he went into the Pharisee's house, and sat down to meat.

37 And, behold, a woman in the city, which was a sinner, when she knew that Jesus sat at meat in the Pharisee's house, brought an alabaster box of ointment,

38 And stood at his feet behind him weeping, and began to wash his feet with tears, and did wipe them with the hairs of her head, and kissed his feet, and anointed them with the ointment.

39 Now when the Pharisee which had bidden him saw it, he spake within himself, saying, This man, if he were a prophet, would have known who and what manner of woman this is that toucheth him: for she is a sinner.

40 And Jesus answering said unto him, Simon, I have somewhat to say unto thee. And he saith, Master, say on.

41 There was a certain creditor which had two debtors: the one owed five hundred pence, and the other fifty.

42 And when they had nothing to pay, he frankly forgave them both. Tell me therefore, which of them will love him most?

43 Simon answered and said, I suppose that he, to whom he forgave most. And he said unto him, Thou hast rightly judged.

44 And he turned to the woman, and said unto Simon, Seest thou this woman? I entered into thine house, thou gavest me no water for my feet: but she hath washed my feet with tears, and wiped them with the hairs of her head.

45 Thou gavest me no kiss: but this woman since the time I came in hath not ceased to kiss my feet.

46 My head with oil thou didst not anoint: but this woman hath anointed my feet with ointment.

47 *Wherefore I say unto thee, Her sins, which are many, are forgiven; for she loved much: but to whom little is forgiven, the same loveth little.*

48 *And he said unto her, Thy sins are forgiven.*

49 *And they that sat at meat with him began to say within themselves, Who is this that forgiveth sins also?*

50 *And he said to the woman, Thy faith hath saved thee; go in peace.*

Teacher's Checklist

Snack Suggestion

Fruit by the Foot
As you enjoy your snack, think of ways that you can show Jesus' love to others.

❑ Read Luke 7:36–50 daily.

❑ Study Lesson Twelve.

❑ Flash cards 12.1–12.3

❑ Purchase snack—Fruit by the Foot.

❑ Print and cut game pieces for "Heart" game.

❑ Print memory verse flash cards from the Ministry Resource CD.

❑ Gather for object lesson—bowl of water, towel, shampoo, baby doll.

❑ Purchase for craft—construction paper and contact paper.

❑ Gather for craft—glue and crayons.

❑ Print and duplicate Coloring Pages or Activity Pages on the Ministry Resource CD (one per student).

❑ Print and duplicate Take-Home Paper on the Ministry Resource CD (one per student).

Bible Lesson

Scripture: Luke 7:36–50

INTRODUCING THE STORY

When you hear the name of a person you know, you automatically think about something in particular from his or her life. You may think about the person's job—"He is a painter." You may think about the person's personality—"She is so funny; she's always telling jokes." You may think about the person's money—"He must be rich." You may think about the person's hobbies—"He's a great ball player." You may think about the person's appearance—"She is the girl with the pretty red hair." You may think about the deeds the person does—"He is always respectful to his parents." You may think about your relationship to the person—"She is my best friend," or "He is my brother."

And there is something people think about when they hear your name. (Teacher, this would be an excellent opportunity for you to build each member of your class, as you share a positive character trait you notice in each of their lives, e.g. "Stephanie, when I think of you, I think of a young lady who is always kind to the people in our church. Benjamin, when I think of you, I think of a young man who is respectful and kind, who always helps me when I need it. Judy, when I think of you, I think of a young lady who always encourages people with a kind word and a smile," etc.)

> **Proverbs 20:11**
>
> 11   Even a child is known by his doings, whether his work be
>   pure, and whether it be right.

In our story from the Bible for today, we will meet a woman who was well known in her city. When people thought of this woman, they didn't think, "She's so kind." They didn't think, "She lives in such a pretty house." They didn't think, "She is such a loving mother." They didn't think any of those things about this woman.

When people thought about the woman in our story, they thought, "She is a sinful woman." When people saw the woman in our story, they thought, "There is that sinful woman." When people talked about the woman in our story, they said, "You know, the woman who lives in sin."

Use an Object

What do you see?
Show pictures of people in various occupations, obvious financial circumstances (rich, poor, etc.), and various performances (playing piano, football, etc.). As you display each picture, ask the students what they notice about the person in the picture. Elicit answers such as, "She is a piano player." "He is a doctor." "They live in a mansion." Point out that each person is known by something others see in his or her life.

Do you know that Jesus thinks differently than we do? Let's find out what Jesus thought about this woman who was known for her sin.

Isaiah 55:8, 9

8   *For my thoughts are not your thoughts, neither are your ways my ways, saith the LORD.*

9   *For as the heavens are higher than the earth, so are my ways higher than your ways, and my thoughts than your thoughts.*

THE STORY

Flash Card 12.1

Teacher's Note

Pharisee: one of a sect among the Jews, whose religion consisted in a strict observance of rites and ceremonies and traditions; their pretended holiness led them to separate themselves, considering themselves more righteous than other Jews

1. Jesus Goes to a Dinner at Simon's House (v. 36)

"I would love to have You come to a special dinner at my house," Simon the Pharisee grandly invited Jesus to a feast.

Now the Pharisees were proud men, thinking they were better than all the other Jews, and, like the rest of the Pharisees, Simon felt superior to other people. The Pharisees thought they were closer to God than other people, because the Pharisees tried very diligently to keep the laws of the Old Testament. They even thought they would go to Heaven because they tried to keep the laws. In fact, the Pharisees were so excited about keeping laws that they even made many extra laws of their own and thought everyone else should live by the laws the Pharisees made.

Jesus knew the Pharisees thought they were better than everyone else. He knew the Pharisees thought the way to go to Heaven was by keeping the laws. He knew the Pharisees made their own laws and expected everyone else to keep them, and that they thought the people who didn't keep the Pharisees' laws didn't deserve to go to Heaven. But, still Jesus loved the Pharisees—just like He loved everyone else in the whole world. And Jesus wanted the Pharisees to know the truth—the truth that it is only through faith—through believing in Jesus, that anyone goes to Heaven.

Normally, in those days, a great fuss was made over guests who would come into one's house. Much of this fuss included activities that we don't see in our culture:

- Since there were no concrete roads or pavement at that time in Israel, travelers' feet would get very dusty as they walked along the dirt roads. Therefore, servants would be on hand to wash the feet of the guest as soon as the guest entered the house.

- In our day, we often hug someone who comes to visit in our home or someone we haven't seen for a long time. When Jesus lived in Israel, it was customary to greet guests with a kiss rather than a hug. It wasn't the kind of kiss we are used to today. The two men (or two women) would touch each other cheek-to-cheek and make a small kissing sound with their lips.

Romans 16:16a

16a Salute one another with an holy kiss.

- An honored guest was often anointed with oil on his head.

Jesus accepted Simon's invitation, and as He entered the house, Simon immediately directed Him as to where He should sit. Jesus took His place on a cushion by the table.

Now, at a special dinner, as this was, the guests didn't sit in chairs as we do today. Instead, they reclined on cushions which were placed on the floor around a low table. They leaned on their left arms and reached for food and ate with their right hands. Their legs were behind them, and if someone were to take a picture of them from above, it would look much like the spokes of a wheel.

2. The Woman Washes Jesus' Feet and Anoints Him (vv. 37–38)

Flash Card 12.2

The well-known woman—the lady whom everyone knew was a sinner—heard that Jesus was eating at Simon's house. She had heard other things about Jesus, too. She had heard that He said He was God the Son. She had heard that when He preached, He said that God loves everyone. She had heard that He healed people of diseases and forgave people of their sins. She had heard that there was no kinder voice and no more loving eyes in the whole world than those of Jesus Christ. "I have to get to this one who will love me and forgive my sin," she said to herself.

When the woman arrived at Simon's house, she was not an invited guest, as were the other people were who were eating with Simon. She was a woman of the city, who was a sinner. And no one wanted her there—well—almost no one.

The woman knew she was not welcome. She saw the dirty looks the other dinner guests gave her, and she knew they were hating her in their hearts. She heard the unkind comments they whispered about her to each other. As she looked into their faces, she saw their eyes which seemed to say, "What is she doing here?!"

But the woman didn't care. "I have to get to Jesus," she thought. "I know who I am. I have lived in sin for many years. I believe in Jesus, and I must go to Him."

The woman didn't think about the other guests anymore. She didn't think about the looks they were giving her, the thoughts they were thinking about her, or the words they were whispering about her. She walked around the table to where Jesus was eating. She opened her bottle of ointment to pour onto His feet, but before she could do so, she thought of her sin. She thought of Jesus, who was God the Son, and that He forgives sin. She became so thankful to Him, and her heart was so full of love for Him, that she began to cry with gratefulness.

"I can't believe it," the woman thought. "Here I am, with God the Son, the forgiver of sins—I, who have been such a great sinner. Oh, I believe Him, and I love Him so much, and I am so thankful that He would forgive even my sins." And the woman cried many tears. As she cried, her tears fell on Jesus' feet, and they mixed in with the dust on His weary feet.

The tears became so many, and Jesus' feet became so wet, that the woman, who had no towel with which to dry Jesus' feet, wiped His wet and dirty feet with her beautiful long hair.

As she dried Jesus' feet, she thought about how good He was to forgive her sin, and she loved Him more than ever. She loved Him with a love that just had to come out, and she began to kiss Jesus' feet.

"Jesus forgives me, a great sinner," the woman thought. "He is so wonderful." And she poured the precious ointment from her bottle onto Jesus' feet.

Flash Card 12.3 — 3. Simon Judges Jesus (v. 39)

Simon couldn't believe what was happening in his own house! He looked at the woman who was washing Jesus' feet with her tears and wiping them with her hair. He smelled the expensive ointment the woman put on Jesus' feet. And Simon felt disgust rising in his heart! He couldn't believe that what he was seeing and what he was smelling was really true.

"If Jesus were a prophet, He would know a person's character—He would know if that person were a righteous person or a sinner," Simon thought to himself. "A prophet ought to at least be able to recognize a sinful person when that person is right there in the same room with Him. Anyone can see that this is a sinful woman who is fallen down at Jesus' feet.

"If Jesus really were a prophet—if He really were sent from God—He would know that this woman is a sinner," Simon thought. "Why, if He were really who He says He is, He wouldn't even let this sinful woman touch Him!"

4. Jesus Knows Simon's Thoughts (v. 40)

Actually, Jesus did know that this woman was a sinner. But because He was God, He could do something even greater than recognizing a sinful person who everyone knew was a sinner. Jesus could recognize sin in a person's heart—even if that person looked good on the outside!

Remember, Simon looked good on the outside, but Jesus knew his heart. Jesus knew exactly what Simon was thinking about the woman, without Simon even saying one word of his thoughts. And Jesus respectfully answered Simon's thoughts, "Simon, I have somewhat to say unto thee." Jesus was going to tell Simon a story to explain the truth, and He waited for Simon to tell Him he wanted to hear the story.

"Master, say on," Simon said. "I am willing to listen to You."

5. Jesus Tells a Story and Asks Simon a Question (vv. 41–42)

Jesus began, "There were two men who each owed a debt to the same moneylender. One man owed fifty pence—the amount he would earn by working at his job for fifty days. The other man owed five hundred pence—the amount he would earn by working at his job for five hundred days!"

Think about it—fifty days is almost two months! And five hundred days! Why, that's almost two years! Think of how long it would take to earn that much money!

"One man owed a lot of money, and the other man owed a lot more money. Each of these two men had a big problem—each man had no money to pay his debt."

Jesus continued, "When it came time for the two men to pay their debts to the moneylender, something happened that they never expected. The moneylender said to each of the debtors, 'I will forgive your debt. You no longer owe me anything.'"

Then Jesus said, "Now, Simon, tell me—which of these two men do you think will love the moneylender the most?" (Teacher, ask your students the same question, allowing them to answer.)

6. Simon's Answer to Jesus (v. 43)

Simon thought for a moment, and then he answered Jesus, "I suppose that he, to whom he forgave most—I imagine the one who owed the most money and was forgiven of his debt would love him the most."

"You have judged rightly," Jesus spoke gently to Simon.

7. Jesus Speaks of the Woman's Love (vv. 44–48)

Then, for the first time, Jesus turned toward the woman as He continued to speak to Simon. Jesus compared the woman's actions with Simon's. "Look at this woman, Simon. Notice what she is doing. You invited Me to your home, and you didn't wash My feet, and you didn't have a servant wash My feet. But this woman has this whole time washed My feet with her tears, and she has wiped them with her hair.

"When I came into your home, you didn't give Me a kiss of greeting. But look at this woman—she has this whole time been kissing My feet.

"When I came into your home, you didn't anoint My head with oil. But this woman has anointed My feet with precious ointment.

"Simon, listen to Me. Yes, she has many sins—like the man who owed five hundred pence to the moneylender. And, just as the man who was forgiven of that huge debt greatly loved the moneylender, this woman greatly loves Me.

"If a person thinks he doesn't have much sin, he won't know he needs to be forgiven, and he won't love very much.

"But when a person knows she is a sinner, then when she is forgiven, she will love very much!"

Teaching Tip

Ask students if they remember one of the cultural customs you mentioned earlier. Point out that Simon did none of these for Jesus when He was a guest in his home.

Then, Jesus spoke the most beautiful words the woman had ever heard. He looked at her with such a true love as she had never before seen, and He said, so everyone in the room could hear, "Your sins are forgiven."

8. The Guests Question Jesus' Credibility (v. 49)

The other guests at the table wondered in their hearts, "How can He forgive sins? Who does He think He is?"

9. Jesus Speaks to the Woman (v. 50)

Jesus had already told the people that He had been sent from God and that He was the Son of God. They knew who He was. So, Jesus spoke to the woman again, so everyone could hear, "It is through your faith that you are saved. Now you can leave with a new peace in your heart."

APPLYING THE STORY

There were two main characters, in addition to Jesus, in our story today. They were the Pharisee and the woman who was known for her sin. They seem to be two very opposite people, and they were. But, in one way, they were exactly alike.

The Pharisee and the woman who was known for her sin were alike in that they were both sinners. They both needed to have their sins forgiven.

But here's what made the greatest difference in the lives of these two sinners: Although the Pharisee was a sinner, he didn't think of himself as a sinner who needed to be forgiven. He didn't look at his sin, didn't think of his sin, and didn't think he needed forgiveness for his sin. Therefore, he didn't love Jesus very much at all.

The woman knew she was a sinner. She looked at her past life and her failures. She knew she needed to be forgiven, and she looked at the forgiveness that Jesus gave her, and she loved Him very much. She was extremely grateful to Jesus.

That is what made the difference in the lives of these two people. One was a sinner who thought about how much Jesus had forgiven her, and the other was a sinner who didn't even think he needed to be forgiven.

We, too, are all sinners who need to have our sins forgiven. Some people, like the woman, sin in ways that everybody else sees and knows about. Other people, like Simon, sin in ways other people don't see—ways such as pride or selfishness.

If we have trusted Jesus as our Saviour, He has forgiven our sins. Just as the woman remembered her sin and thought about how much Jesus had done for her, we need to remind ourselves of what Jesus has done for us.

Jesus loves us more than any other person ever has or ever will love us. He loves us so much that He came to Earth and died on the cross to pay the price for our sins so we wouldn't have to. And, even after we have trusted Him as our Saviour, we still sin, and He still forgives us.

1 John 1:9

9   *If we confess our sins, he is faithful and just to forgive us our sins, and to cleanse us from all unrighteousness.*

When we think of who we are and who Jesus is and what He has done for us, we will love Him like the woman did. We will love Him so much that we will want to show our love for Him in every way we can.

What will love for Jesus look like in your lives? How can you show your love for the Lord Jesus? (Wait for responses.)

When you love Jesus like the woman in our story loved Jesus, you will want to tell Him that you love Him. Have you told Jesus that you love Him today? Have you sung songs of praise to Him?

Psalm 100:2

2   *Serve the LORD with gladness: come before his presence with singing.*

When you love Jesus like the woman in our story loved Jesus, your heart will want to thank Him for what He does for you. Have you thanked Jesus today? He has done so much for each one of us.

Psalm 103:1–2

1   *Bless the LORD, O my soul: and all that is within me, bless his holy name.*

2   *Bless the LORD, O my soul, and forget not all his benefits*

When you love Jesus like the woman in our story loved Jesus, you will be loyal to Him—you will speak up for Him when others say they don't believe in Him or when they say He isn't good. Have you spoken up for Jesus?

When you love Jesus like the woman in our story loved Jesus, you will want to spend time with Him. Have you spent time with Him today?

When you love Jesus like the woman in our story loved Jesus, you will want to give to Jesus, just as she gave her oil. What can you give to Jesus? (Allow students to respond.)

- Tithe
- Offering
- Time (singing in choir, cleaning the church, helping your family at home, writing a note to someone who needs encouragement, etc.)
- Giving to others

Matthew 25:40

40   *And the King shall answer and say unto them, Verily I say unto you, Inasmuch as ye have done it unto one of the least of these my brethren, ye have done it unto me.*

The woman's love for Jesus came from a heart that was grateful for how much she had been forgiven. We have all been forgiven of our sins that caused Jesus to have to die on the cross. When we think of what He has done for us, our grateful hearts will cause us to show our love to Him, too.

Review Game/Questions

Heart

Materials Needed
Game pieces from the Ministry Resource CD

Set Up
Print and cut games pieces.

Playing the Game
Place game pieces in a bag. Ask students a question. If the answer is correct, the student will draw a card from the bag. If the card drawn is a point card (whole heart), the student may continue drawing, or stop with the points he or she has. The student can stop at anytime. But, if a half heart is drawn, then the student loses all points accumulated up to that point and his or her turn is over. The student with the most points is the winner!

1. Who invited Jesus to dinner at his house?
   Answer: Simon the Pharisee

2. What were the Pharisees like?
   Answer: They were proud. They thought they were better than everyone. They thought they were closer to God and would go to Heaven because they tried to keep all of the laws. They even made extra laws of their own.

3. Was the well-known, sinful woman an invited guest at Simon's home that day?
   Answer: No.

4. When this sinful woman saw Jesus, what did she do?
   Answer: She cried. She wiped His feet with her hair, kissed His feet, and anointed them with ointment.

5. What did Simon think to himself when he saw the woman act this way toward Jesus?
   Answer: He thought, "If Jesus were a prophet, He would know that this woman is a sinner."

6. Did Jesus answer Simon's words or his thoughts?
   Answer: Jesus knew what Simon was thinking and answered his thoughts.

7. What reason did Jesus give for the woman's extravagant actions?
    Answer: Jesus said the woman did all these things because she loved Him.

8. Did Simon show any love or respect to Jesus when He entered his home?
    Answer: No, Simon did not wash His feet or give a kiss of greeting.

9. What did Jesus say to the woman at the end of the story?
    Answer: "Thy faith hath saved thee. Go in peace."

10. What was the greatest difference between the two sinners (the woman and the Pharisee) in our story?
    Answer: The woman recognized her need for forgiveness. The Pharisee didn't think of himself as a sinner in need of forgiveness.

 # Teaching the Memory Verse

Mark 12:30

30 *And thou shalt love the Lord thy God with all thy heart, and with all thy soul, and with all thy mind, and with all thy strength: this is the first commandment.*

Print flash cards from the Ministry Resource CD.

When we love the one true God with all our hearts, God becomes the center of our lives and is first in everything!

Choose six students to come to the front of the class. Give each student a flash card to hold. Stand behind the first student. While standing behind the student, the class will say the phrase on the flash card. When you move to another flash card the class will say that phrase. For example: Stand behind the reference flash card. The class will repeat Mark 12:30 until you move on to "and thou shalt love the Lord thy God with all thy heart." Stand behind that flash card until class has repeated phrase about three times, then move behind flash card one. Then move to flash card two, three, and then back to one. Continue with all six flash cards.

Object Lesson—Showing Jesus' Love

Materials Needed:
- Bowl of water
- Towel
- Shampoo
- Baby doll

For the Teacher:

Take the shampoo and poor it into a nice looking container or decorate the shampoo bottle to make the bottle look expensive. Before class begins, wet the feet of the doll and put sand or dirt on the feet.

Tell the class:

Explain to the children that inside this bottle is very important and expensive ointment. Ask the children, "What do you think needs to be washed on this doll?" The feet. Remind the children that this ointment cost a lot of money. Have one child come up and help you to begin washing the feet of the baby doll.

Explain to the children that in Bible days everyone wore sandals, and this caused their feet to become dirty very quickly. The people of the day would wash their feet often to keep them clean. The dirtiest part of someone's body, in those days, was their feet.

People would wash someone else's feet for them to show how much they loved and cared for them. Washing someone's feet would show that you were lowering yourself to do something nice for them. The lady that washed Jesus' feet gave a very expensive ointment to Jesus and showed that she loved Him very much. What do we do to show Jesus that we love Him?

Craft—Kids Placemat

Getting It Together

Construction paper

Glue

Crayons

Contact paper

Per Student:

1   Placemat template from the Ministry Resource CD

Putting It Together

1.   Have students color the placemat.
2.   Glue to a piece of construction paper.
3.   Cover with contact paper or laminate.

Seeing It Together

Once the placemat is finished, have each student make a list of ways to show God's love to others.

Additional Resources

Find the following items on the Ministry Resource CD:

•   Coloring Page (for younger children)

•   Activity Page (for older children)

•   Student Take-Home Paper

•   PowerPoint Presentation

Suggested Classroom Schedule

Before Class	Complete attendance record. Provide students with coloring pages/activity pages.
Opening	Welcome
Prayer	Prayer requests and praise reports from the children
Song Time	
Memory Verse	Hebrews 11:6
Song Time	
Object Lesson	Make Jesus BIG!
Bible Lesson	The People in Nazareth Don't Believe
Application/Invitation	Help saved students apply lesson. Invite unsaved students to receive Christ.
Snack	Patriotic Cupcakes
Review Game/ Questions	Lifesavers
Craft	Bookmark
Closing	Give announcements and pray. Distribute take-home papers.

Lesson Thirteen Overview

The People in Nazareth

Theme—Only faith in Jesus allows us to see miracles.

Scripture

Mark 6:1–6

Memory Verse

Hebrews 11:6 —*"But without faith it is impossible to please him: for he that cometh to God must believe that he is, and that he is a rewarder of them that diligently seek him."*

Lesson Outline

Introducing the Story

Today's story is about Jesus going back to His hometown. Let's find out what the people thought of Jesus when He returned.

Telling the Story

1. **Jesus Visits His Hometown of Nazareth** (v. 1) —*Flash Card 13.1*

2. **Jesus Teaches and the People Are Astonished** (v. 2) —*Flash Card 13.2*

3. **The People Are Offended** (v. 3)

4. **Jesus Acknowledges Rejection** (v. 4, Acts 7:52)

5. **Their Lack of Faith Limited Miracles in Their Town** (v. 5, Matthew 17:20)

6. **Jesus Marvels at Their Unbelief** (v. 6)—*Flash Card 13.3*

Applying the Story (Hebrews 11:6, Ephesians 3:20, Psalm 34:18a, Psalm 27:10, 46:1, 119:169b, 1 Peter 2:23, Philippians 4:19)

Have you been going to Jesus in faith? You cannot imagine what miracles He will do in your life if you live a life of faith.

13 Lesson Thirteen

The People in Nazareth Don't Believe

Theme: Only faith in Jesus allows us to see miracles.

 Scripture

Mark 6:1–6

1   And he went out from thence, and came into his own country; and his disciples follow him.

2   And when the sabbath day was come, he began to teach in the synagogue: and many hearing him were astonished, saying, From whence hath this man these things? and what wisdom is this which is given unto him, that even such mighty works are wrought by his hands?

3   Is not this the carpenter, the son of Mary, the brother of James, and Joses, and of Juda, and Simon? and are not his sisters here with us? And they were offended at him.

4   But Jesus, said unto them, A prophet is not without honour, but in his own country, and among his own kin, and in his own house.

5   And he could there do no mighty work, save that he laid his hands upon a few sick folk, and healed them.

6   And he marvelled because of their unbelief. And he went round about the villages, teaching.

Memory Verse

Hebrews 11:6
"But without faith it is impossible to please him: for he that cometh to God must believe that he is, and that he is a rewarder of them that diligently seek him."

Teacher's Checklist

❑ Read Mark 6:1–6 daily.

❑ Study Lesson Thirteen.

❑ Flash cards 13.1–13.3

❑ Prepare snack—Patriotic Cupcakes.

❑ Print "Lifesavers" game from Ministry Resource CD.

❑ Purchase lifesavers for review game.

❑ Print and cut out memory verse visual.

❑ Purchase for memory verse—magnetic strip or Velcro.

❑ Gather for object lesson—magnifying glass.

❑ Purchase for craft—foam stickers and bookmark.

❑ Print verse template for craft from the Ministry Resource CD.

❑ Print and duplicate Coloring Pages or Activity Pages on the Ministry Resource CD (one per student).

❑ Print and duplicate Take-Home Paper on the Ministry Resource CD (one per student).

Snack Suggestion

Patriotic Cupcakes
Serve patriotic-themed cupckaes and explain the burden Jesus had to see His own country believe in Him.

Bible Lesson

Scripture: Mark 6:1–6

INTRODUCING THE STORY

We all have neighbors—people who live close to us. Your neighbors might be the "grandma-and-grandpa" type neighbors. Maybe when you visit them, they like to tell you stories about when they were young, and maybe they give you cookies and a glass of milk.

Maybe your neighbors are a younger family with a child your age. Maybe you like to go to their house to play, or they come to your house to play. Maybe you walk to school together.

Perhaps your neighbors are a couple with no children, or maybe a single man or woman is your neighbor.

Your neighbors have all different kinds of jobs. One neighbor might be a teacher, another a plumber, and another a factory worker. Your neighbor may be a dentist, a farmer, or an electrician.

Tell me about your neighbors. (Allow various children to describe different aspects of their neighbors.) How do you think your neighbors would describe you to me if I were to ask them to tell me about you? (Again, allow students to answer.)

Do you know that, although you may know a lot about your neighbors, and your neighbors might know a lot about you, there are many things you don't know about each other? You may know the names of each other's family members, but neither of you knows what the other thinks about when he or she is alone. You may know the color of each other's hair and eyes, but you don't know about all the books the other has read and the knowledge the other has stored up to be used when he or she is grown.

The Lord Jesus Christ had neighbors when He was growing up in the city of Nazareth.

It was in Nazareth that Jesus spent His childhood and teenage years. Nazareth is the town where Jesus worked with His earthly dad, Joseph, in the carpentry shop, learning how to be a carpenter.

If we had asked Jesus' neighbors to tell us about Him as a young boy or teenager, they would have thought they knew all about Him, just as your neighbors may think they know all about you. They would likely have said things like, "His dad is a carpenter, and Jesus helps him in the shop," or "I know Him—His brothers, James and Simon, are my best friends." They may have said,

"I had a great time fishing with Him in the Sea of Galilee." One of His neighbors might say, "He's a great guy—one time He helped me build a neat little bench, and I gave it to my mom for her birthday."

But the truth is, Jesus' neighbors in Nazareth really did not know who Jesus was. To them, Jesus was just another kid growing up in their town, but in today's true story from the Bible, Jesus reveals to them who He really is— the Messiah, the Son of God, God Himself, the Saviour of the world.

And this really troubled them—the people of Nazareth who had watched Jesus grow up, and who thought they knew who He was. It wasn't the fact that they would have to admit, "Oh, maybe we don't know Him as well as we thought we did" that troubled them. What troubled the people of Nazareth was that now they would have to admit, "Oh, I guess I don't know myself as well as I thought I did. If I believe that Jesus is the Messiah, the Saviour of the world, I will have to admit that I am a sinner, needing to be forgiven."

Let's find out what happened to these people who didn't know Jesus as well as they had thought they knew Him.

THE STORY

Flash Card 13.1

1. Jesus Visits His Hometown of Nazareth (v. 1)

Jesus had been teaching and healing people close to the Sea of Galilee, about twenty miles from Nazareth, the town where He had grown up. There, by the Sea of Galilee, Jesus had performed two amazing miracles:

He healed a woman who had been very sick for twelve long years. She had gone from doctor to doctor and spent all of her money, but she didn't get any better. In fact, she just kept getting sicker! In a huge crowd of people, she reached out and touched the hem of Jesus' robe, and she was healed!

He raised a twelve-year-old girl from the dead—she wasn't just sick, she didn't just have a headache or a stomachache—but she was actually dead! Jesus brought her back to life!

After performing these two miracles, and many others, Jesus came back to His hometown of Nazareth. The people in Nazareth had likely heard about all these miracles Jesus had done, and they were all excited.

Somebody had likely returned from the Sea of Galilee to Nazareth and said, "Hey did you hear? Jesus healed a lady who had been sick for twelve years. She had gone from doctor to doctor, and she had spent all her money, but none of the doctors could make her any better—she only got worse. But Jesus healed her completely!"

Somebody else might have said, "Not only that, Jesus raised a twelve-year-old girl from the dead. I mean, she had actually died. I was there—I saw it myself. We were all wailing and weeping and crying. Jesus walks up and says, 'Don't worry about it. She's just asleep.' We all laughed at Him. Then Jesus calls His disciples, Peter, James and John, and her mom and dad to come with Him. He says to the rest of us, 'All right, everybody else stay out here.' And He goes into the room with the girl and shuts the door. And there He is, in the room with this dead girl. Now, I have to tell you, I didn't know what was going to happen, but I was curious. So I creep up to the door, and I put my ear to the door so I can hear what's going on. I hear Jesus say, 'Damsel, I say unto thee, Arise.' And the next thing I know, the door opens, she walks out, and Jesus says, 'Give her something to eat.' It was amazing—one moment she's dead, and the next moment she's sitting there, eating. And guess what? Jesus is on His way here now—to Nazareth! Can you believe it?"

And as the man was speaking, someone in the crowd called out, "Oh, here He is now—see Him coming down the path. And, look, His disciples are with Him. Wow, that's a lucky bunch to be able to travel with Jesus!"

2. Jesus Teaches and the People Are Astonished (v. 2)

Flash Card 13.2

Now when the Sabbath day came, Jesus went into the synagogue and began to teach the people about God. And many of the people of the town of Nazareth were astonished. They were amazed with Jesus. They were amazed for two reasons:

Because of what He said. They could see that Jesus spoke with great wisdom. They hadn't realized Jesus had such wisdom when He was a young boy growing up in Nazareth. In fact, as they listened to Him now, they asked, "What wisdom is this which is given unto Him?"

Because of what He did. They were amazed at the miracles He performed. The same people who spoke of His wisdom said also, "Even such mighty works are wrought by His hands."

Teacher's Note

The Sabbath Day was the special day God chose for the Jews in the Old Testament to rest and thank God for His goodness.

3. The People Are Offended (v. 3)

So here they were, really impressed with Jesus, amazed at what He said. But then someone said, "Hey, isn't this the carpenter? Sure, and His mom is Mary.

We watched Him grow up here, just down the street, with the rest of His brothers and sisters!"

And these same people who were so impressed with His wisdom and miracles became offended at Him—they were displeased and angry with Him. They thought, "How could this little kid who grew up in our own town now become our teacher and leader?"

4. Jesus Acknowledges Rejection (v. 4)

As Jesus heard their words and knew their thoughts, He realized that these people who had accepted Him at the beginning were now rejecting Him. He looked at the crowd and said, "A prophet is often rejected by those of his hometown—by the people of his own community, by his relatives, and even by his own family."

It had always been that way. When God, in the Old Testament, sent prophets to the people to warn them that they were going the wrong way, doing the wrong things, and disobeying God, the people often rejected the prophets, sometimes even killing them.

> **Acts 7:52**
>
> 52   Which of the prophets have not your fathers persecuted? and they have slain them which shewed before of the coming of the Just One; of whom ye have been now the betrayers and murderers.

And now, the people were rejecting Jesus—the one who had come to save them from their sins.

5. Their Lack of Faith Limited Miracles in Their Town (v. 5)

Remember the twelve-year-old girl whom Jesus had brought back to life? Before she had died, her father had gone to Jesus, begging Him to heal his daughter, believing that Jesus could heal his daughter. And, when his daughter died, Jesus told the man, "Be not afraid, only believe" (Mark 5:36). And the man believed Jesus, and Jesus raised his daughter from the dead. Jesus brought the man's daughter back to life because the man had faith.

Matthew 17:20

20 *And Jesus said unto them, Because of your unbelief: for verily I say unto you, If ye have faith as a grain of mustard seed, ye shall say unto this mountain, Remove hence to yonder place; and it shall remove; and nothing shall be impossible unto you.*

Remember the woman who had been sick for twelve years and had gone to many doctors? Remember how the doctors hadn't been able to cure her disease, but she had only gotten sicker? When Jesus healed her, He said, "Daughter, thy faith hath made thee whole" (Mark 5:34). Jesus healed the woman because she had faith.

But here in Nazareth, most of the people didn't believe Jesus. Most of the people of Jesus' hometown didn't have faith. Their lack of faith kept Jesus from being able to do wonderful miracles in Nazareth like He had done by the Sea of Galilee and other places He had been.

To be sure, there were a lot of sick people in Nazareth when Jesus came to preach. In fact, a few of them had faith, and Jesus healed those few people. But, sadly, there were still a lot of sick people in Nazareth when Jesus left. Not many of the sick people in Nazareth were healed. The people of Nazareth were not helped much by Jesus coming to them, because they didn't believe—they didn't have faith.

6. Jesus Marvels at Their Unbelief (v. 6)   Flash Card 13.3

In the many places where Jesus traveled, there were many people Jesus met who had faith. In fact, Jesus marveled because of the faith of one man. A ruler came to Jesus to ask Him to heal the ruler's servant, and Jesus marveled at his faith (Matthew 8:10).

And in today's story, Jesus marveled again. It was not the faith of the people that caused Jesus to marvel this time—it was their lack of faith. "And he marvelled because of their unbelief."

The unbelief of the people caused Jesus to not be able to heal their sick. The unbelief of the people caused Jesus to not be able to raise any dead people. Worst of all, the unbelief of the people kept them from trusting Jesus as their Saviour from sin.

And so Jesus went on His way, preaching and teaching in other places.

APPLYING THE STORY

Jesus was sorrowful over the unbelief of the people of His own hometown. "It is the people's unbelief that makes it so I can't do great miracles here like I have done by the Sea of Galilee and the other places to which I have traveled," He must have thought. "They have great needs, just like all the other people I have helped. If only they would believe, they could see great miracles. God the Father wants to do so much in their lives. If only they had faith."

It's the same in your life. Jesus wants to do great things for you. He knows your needs, and He wants to fill those needs. But He won't force Himself upon you. He will work in your life through your faith—through your believing in Him. He waits for us to come to Him in faith.

> **Hebrews 11:6**
>
> 6   *But without faith it is impossible to please him: for he that cometh to God must believe that he is, and that he is a rewarder of them that diligently seek him.*

What is your need? What problem do you have in your life that you know you can't solve on your own?

- Is your heart full of pain because someone you love has died?
- Are you hurting inside because your parents have gotten a divorce?
- Are you sick?
- Are you having problems with your schoolwork?
- Has your friend treated you unkindly, and now you feel angry or lonely?
- Has your dad lost his job, and you worry about how your family will have enough money?

God says when you come to Him in faith, He will do amazing miracles in your life.

> **Ephesians 3:20**
>
> 20   *Now unto him that is able to do exceeding abundantly above all that we ask or think, according to the power that worketh in us.*

What God does in our lives when we come to Him in faith is even better than we think it will be.

When you lose a loved one and, with a broken heart, you go to God in faith, He miraculously comforts your heart and fills you with peace and joy.

Psalm 34:18a

18a The LORD is nigh unto them that are of a broken heart

When you hurt inside because your parents have gotten a divorce or one of them has left your family, and you go to God in faith, He will miraculously be there for you.

Psalm 27:10

10 When my father and my mother forsake me, then the LORD will take me up.

When you are sick and you go to God in faith, He may miraculously heal your body. If He chooses to heal your body, or if He chooses not to heal your body, He will miraculously bless your faith by reminding you that He is always your helper, whether you are sick or well.

Psalm 46:1

1 God is our refuge and strength, a very present help in trouble.

When you are having problems with your schoolwork, and you go to God in faith, He will miraculously open up your understanding through His Word.

Psalm 119:169b

169b Give me understanding according to thy word

When someone has treated you unkindly, and you go to God in faith, He will miraculously comfort you, reminding you that He, also, was treated unkindly. He will teach you how to love those who hurt you.

1 Peter 2:23

23 Who, when he was reviled, reviled not again; when he suffered, he threatened not; but committed himself to him that judgeth righteously

When your dad has lost his job, and you go to God in faith, He will miraculously provide for you, His child.

Philippians 4:19

19 But my God shall supply all your need according to his
riches in glory by Christ Jesus.

Jesus is still the miracle-worker. But He does His greatest miracles in the lives of those who have faith in Him.

Maybe the problem you have in your life is your sin. Maybe you, like the people of Nazareth, have never trusted Jesus as your own Saviour from sin. Jesus came to Earth over two thousand years ago just for you. He came to pay the price for your sin. He is the only one Who is able to save you from your sin.

I will be available after class to explain to you how you can take your sin problem to Jesus so He can miraculously forgive your sin and make you His child.

Jesus was amazed at faith—He was amazed at some because of their great faith, and He was amazed at some because of their lack of faith. He miraculously worked in the lives of those with faith, and He could do no miracles in the lives of those without faith.

He wants you to come to Him in faith. You cannot imagine what miracles He will do in your life.

 ## Review Game/Questions

Lifesavers

Set up

Print game sheet on cardstock. Laminate for durability. Purchase individually wrapped lifesavers (original flavor) and place in a non see-through bag.

Playing the Game

Divide class into teams. Ask a student a review question. If the answer is correct, allow the student to draw a candy from the bag. Match the candy color to the candy color on the game card. Award his or her team the corresponding points. The student gets to keep the candy.

1. What was the name of Jesus' hometown?
    Answer: Nazareth

2. What had Jesus just done near the Sea of Galilee before He traveled to Nazareth?
    Answer: He had just performed two miracles of healing.

3. What was the Sabbath Day?
    Answer: It was a special day God chose for the Jews to rest and remember Him.

4. What did Jesus do in Nazareth on the Sabbath day?
    Answer: He taught about God in the synagogue.

5. What first reaction did the people of Jesus' town have when He taught?
    Answer: They were amazed.

6. Why were the people of Nazareth amazed?
    Answer: They were amazed because of what Jesus said. They were amazed because of what Jesus did.

7. What was the second reaction the people of Nazareth had?
    Answer: They were offended.

8. Why couldn't Jesus do any miracles in His hometown of Nazareth?
    Answer: Because the people rejected Him and did not believe in Him.

9. What do we need to have in order for Jesus to do miracles for us?
    Answer: We need to have faith.

10. What are some amazing miracles God can do in your life?
    Answer: Answers may vary, but could include examples given on page 208.

Teaching the Memory Verse

Hebrews 11:6

6   *But without faith it is impossible to please him: for he that cometh to God must believe that he is, and that he is a rewarder of them that diligently seek him.*

Print and cut out Hebrews 11:6. Laminate for durability and put either a magnetic strip or piece of Velcro on back of each piece. Place all pieces on board in random order (scattered, not in a straight line).

Ask students to open to Hebrews 11:6. Have students repeat the reference. Then add one phrase at a time and repeat.

But without faith—we cannot see faith. Faith is confident obedience to God's Word regardless of circumstances and consequences.

It is impossible to please him—we cannot please God in any other way.

For he that cometh to God must believe that he is—God is the source of all being, all powerful.

And that he is a rewarder of them that diligently seek him—If I want to be rewarded by the Lord, then I must seek Him and what He wants.

Now ask one student to come to the board and place the picture card that comes first in our memory verse today. Then ask another student to come forward and place the second picture for our verse. Continue adding a picture at a time until the entire verse is in order.

Object Lesson—Make Jesus BIG!

Materials Needed:

Magnifying glass

Lesson:

Allow the children to use the magnifying glass and pass it around. Hold it in front of your eye and show them it makes things bigger. Jesus was walking around healing people, and the people in those villages didn't think much of it. Jesus was not a big deal to them. Jesus should be the biggest person in our lives. He has allowed us to get saved, allowed us to have a church to attend and blessed us in a great way. Make Jesus really BIG in your life.

Craft—Bookmark

Getting It Together

Foam stickers

Per student:
1 Foam bookmark
1 Verse template from the Ministry
Resource CD

Putting It Together

1. Using foam letters, have students spell out the word FAITH.
2. Decorate with sticker shapes.
3. Glue the verse template on the back.

Seeing It Together

When you place your faith in Jesus, He will allow you to see miracles. Encourage each student to read the memory verse and remember to trust Jesus each day!

Additional Resources

Find the following items on the Ministry Resource CD:

• Coloring Page (for younger children)

• Activity Page (for older children)

• Student Take-Home Paper

• PowerPoint Presentation

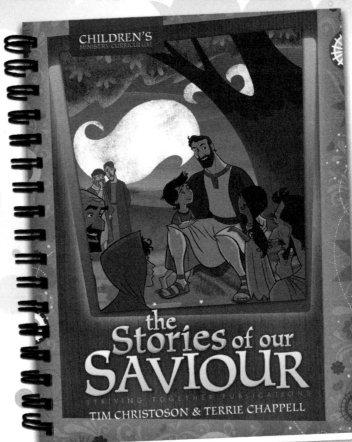